Henry Grady
or
Tom Watson?

The Rhetorical Struggle for the New South, 1880–1890

The publication of this book
is made possible through a generous grant from
the Watson-Brown Foundation, Inc.,
Thomson, Georgia.

Henry Grady or Tom Watson?

The Rhetorical Struggle for the New South, 1880–1890

Ferald J. Bryan.

Mercer University Press
Macon, Georgia
1994

ISBN 0-86554-439-5

Henry Grady or Tom Watson?
The Rhetorical Struggle for the New South,
1880–1890

by Ferald J. Bryan

Copyright © 1994
Mercer University Press, Macon, Georgia 31207 USA

The paper used in this publication meets the minimum requirements
of American National Standard for Information Sciences—
Permanence of Paper for Printed Library Materials,
ANSI Z39.48-1984.

Library of Congress Cataloging-in-Publication Data

Bryan, Ferald J.
Henry Grady or Tom Watson?: The Rhetorical Struggle for the New
    South, 1880–1890/ Ferald J. Bryan
    viii + 167 pp.   6 x 9"
    Includes bibliographical reference and index.
    ISBN 0-86554-439-5
1. Grady, Henry.   2. Watson, Tom.   3. Georgia—History.
    4. Georgia—History—19th century.   5. Oratory—Southern.
I. Bryan, Ferald J.   II. Title.

                                        94-25517
                                        CIP

Table of Contents

Preface vii

Introduction 1
  A Survey of Southern Oratory 3
  This Study of Henry Grady and Tom Watson 10

Chapter
  1. The Southern Mind and Metaphor 17
    The Southern Mind and Agriculture 18
    Southern Religious Rhetoric and Economic Recovery 20
    Southern Religion, Rhetoric, and Metaphor 24
    The Early Life of Henry W. Grady 32
    The Early Life of Thomas E. Watson 34

  2. Henry Grady's Vision 39
    Grady Matures as Editor and Speaker 39
    The New South Speech 44
    Grady's Dallas Speech 47
    The Farmer's Place: Grady's Speeches for
      Agrarian Reform 52
    Grady's Final Speeches 57
    Grady's Metaphors: The Vision Unified 60

  3. Tom Watson's Vision 63
    Matures as Attorney and Speaker 64
    The Mature Epideictic: Watson's Speeches, 1883-1886 . . . 70
    An Aggressive Epideictic: Watson's Speeches, 1888-1889 . 76
    Watson's Metaphors: The Vision Unified 87

  4. Through the Matrix of Metaphors 89
    Setting the Stage: Metaphors and Remembrance
      of Things Past 90
    A New Truth Revealed: Metaphors and the Future 92
    Metaphors and Southern Identity 96

Appendix A : Key Speeches of Henry Grady 99

    Grady's New South Speech 99

    Grady's The Farmer and the Cities Speech at Elberton,
        Georgia 108

Appendix B: Key Speeches of Tom Watson 125

    Watson's Commencement Address at Mercer University 125

    Watson's Commencement Address at Milledgeville,
        Georgia 141

Selected Bibliography 155

Index 163

Preface

This book is written for those who believe in the power of the spoken word. In ancient Greece and Rome, future societal leaders studied first in the liberal arts then carefully in the practice of rhetoric and oratory. The young students spent many hours reviewing the great model speeches from Pericles, Demosthenes, and Cicero so they could master the skills necessary to move the masses. Greek and Roman society believed in the power of oratory to lead their people toward a greater future.

The American South of the eighteenth and nineteenth century tried to model its view of leadership on classical Greek and Roman culture. When the Civil War decided the issues of slavery and states rights, traditional Southern society was left adrift with few cultural anchors. One of the pillars of Southern culture, respect for oratory, helped lead Southerners toward a hopeful future in the midst of economic and social destruction. Henry Grady and Tom Watson were two of the key orators that grew up in the oral tradition of the South and relied upon this tradition to move their audiences toward their own personal visions of success.

This book analyzes the rhetorical struggle between Watson and Grady during the critical decade of the 1880s. For the most part, the speeches of Grady and Watson are allowed to stand on their own. The tools of historical and rhetorical criticism are employed to help place Grady and Watson within the unique context that allowed them to practice their oratorical skills to such an effective level.

I am grateful for the help of so many of my friends and colleagues in making this book possible. The Department of Communication Studies at Northern Illinois University provided release time from my teaching duties to allow me to complete this manuscript. My Department Chair, Richard L. Johannesen, has provided constant support and encouragement for my rhetorical efforts for many years. I am also thankful for the support of Dorothy Bishop, Martha Cooper, Clifton Cornwell, Winifred Horner, Charles Larson, Jackson Lears, Jack Parker, Lois Self, and Charles Tucker.

I am also very appreciative of the advice and support provided this project by Tom Watson Brown, great grandson of Tom Watson. Finally, I am especially grateful for the love, support, and inspiration of my son, Caleb Daniel Bryan.

Ferald J. Bryan
DeKalb, Illinois

Dedication

This book is dedicated to the memory of my grandfathers, Henry Grady Bryan and William Allen Hinton, whose stories of their struggles growing up in the South provided the true genesis of my perspective on Southern oratory.

Introduction

"There was a South of slavery and secession—that South is dead. There
is a South of union and freedom—that South, thank God, is living,
breathing, growing every hour."
—Benjamin H. Hill
quoted by Henry W. Grady
"The New South"

"That old Southern homestead was a little kingdom, a complete social
and industrial organism, almost wholly sufficient unto itself, asking less
of the outer world than it gave. How sound, sane, healthy it appears,
even now, when compared to certain phases of certain other systems!"
—Tom Watson
Bethany

During the historical era immediately following the War Between the
States, the people of the American South confronted a period of great
introspection. After Federal troops finally withdrew from most Southern
states in 1880, the South faced an uncertain future. The agricultural base
that had provided the foundation for the Southern economy lay in complete shambles. Historian John D. Hicks has observed that the South returned to economic conditions so "primitive" that it reminded one of the
early frontier.[1]

To combat the growing sense of regional disorientation, numerous
spokesmen took to the stump in an attempt to lead the South toward a
more optimistic future. The tendency for most Southerners to reach out
for leaders offering hope for the defeated region peaked in the 1880s.
According to George Tindall, the white Southerner longed for orators
who could build "mind pictures of his world or of the larger world
around him . . . images of perfection" that would permit the defeat in the
past to be forgotten.[2] The need for speakers to comfort the broken spirit

---

[1]John D. Hicks, *The Populist Revolt* (Lincoln: University of Nebraska Press, 1961)
37.

[2]George B. Tindall, *Romance and Realism in Southern Politics* (Athens: University
of Georgia Press, 1961) 17-18.

of the South quickly evolved into an important cultural ritual. Since before the war, Waldo Braden notes, "Southerners had long heard their preachers and politicians tell them they were superior, a 'chosen people'."[3] Braden argues that as a "defeated people," Southerners looked for a soothing "balm for their bruised ego's."[4] Orator Henry Woodfin Grady provided his fellow Southerners with a new romantic image of their past and future, and they found relief in his comforting rhetoric.

As editor of the influential *Atlanta Constitution*, Henry Grady regarded himself as a prophet whose mission was the "uplifting and rebuilding of the prostrate and bleeding South."[5] The image that Grady offered contained keen wit and figures of speech or word pictures that emotionalized his audiences.[6] Grady's goal was to become the main spokesman for the South's aspiring post-war business class and to spread a gospel of a New South of industrialization.[7]

The leadership that Grady offered through his rhetoric in the 1880s, however, was not the only persuasive image of the South's future being articulated. Thomas Edward Watson, a fellow Georgian from Thomson, challenged the progressive vision of Grady from a traditional agrarian perspective. C. Vann Woodward contends that "Watson never did embrace" the New South creed for his own.[8] Instead, Watson also took to the stump and became the "embodiment of the new rebellion" against Grady's position in Georgia and throughout the South.[9] With these two competing visions being formulated and forcefully delivered during the 1880s, Woodward has identified this period as a study of the divided mind in the South.[10]

-----

[3]Waldo W. Braden, "Repining Over an Irrevocable Past: The Ceremonial Orator in a Defeated Society," in *Rhetoric of the People*, ed. Barret, 274.

[4]Ibid., 274-75.

[5]As quoted in Mills Lane, ed. *The New South: Writings and Speeches of Henry Grady* (Savannah: The Beehive Press, 1971) vii-viii.

[6]Charles F. Lindsley, "Henry Woodfin Grady, Orator," *Quarterly Journal of Speech Education* 6 (April 1920): 30-31.

[7]Lane, vii.

[8]C. Vann Woodward, *Tom Watson: Agrarian Rebel* (London: Oxford University Press, 1938) 114.

[9]Ibid., 126-27.

[10]C. Vann Woodward, *Origins of the New South* (Baton Rouge: Louisiana State University Press, 1951) 142-45.

A Survey of Southern Oratory

Most Southerners tended to view this intense public debate within the broad oral tradition that had marked much of their earlier social and cultural heritage. Rollin Osterweis notes that oratory in the Old South was an "end in itself . . . the key to power in society."[11]Since Southerners considered public discourse an important cultural event, two well-respected orators could make a difference with their rhetoric.

Given the abundance of evidence that Grady and Watson formed the rhetorical battlelines that influenced the symbolic future of the South, it is surprising how few scholars of rhetoric and public address have studied these two rhetors. A few studies of Watson's and Grady's persuasive strategies do exist, but most of these tend to be limited Neo-Aristotelian efforts that only try to gauge each individual speaker's effectiveness. Paul Gaston, for example, has carefully investigated Grady's discourse as a powerful mythmaking enterprise at the turn of the century.[12] But as an intellectual historian, Gaston was more concerned with how, in the aftermath of Grady's speeches and early death, a new mythic "creed of salvation" arose and how diverse and pervasive the new creed had become by the beginning of World War Two.

Past scholars have tended to consign Grady and Watson to the demonstrative oratorical genre and thus fail to account for the discourse *itself* as an important rhetorical phenomenon, unfolding within a region of the country uniquely attuned to the oral tradition.[13] Just as it is proper for a political or social historian to explain the past in terms of situations controlled by political or social forces, it is the role of the rhetorical historian (including the historian of public address) to explain the past in terms of situations or events whose key forces are rhetorical. Rhetorical forms are the uniquely human communicative impulses and the circumstances, material and symbolic, which fuel or impede those impulses. The rhetorical act and symbol are central among the forces (economic,

---

[11]Rollin G. Osterweis, *Romanticism and Nationalism in the Old South* (New Haven: Yale University Press, 1949) 94-95.

[12]Paul M. Gaston, *The New South Creed: A Study in Mythmaking* (Baton Rouge: Louisiana State University Press, 1976).

[13]Waldo W. Braden, *The Oral Tradition in the South* (Baton Rouge: Louisiana State University Press, 1983).

political, social) which drive and define the flow of history. While scholars in the fields of speech communication and American history have
produced a sizable body of literature on both Grady and Watson, no
study has compared their oratory as vital to the South.

The earliest treatment of Tom Watson's rhetoric in speech communication literature was hardly flattering. Robert Gunderson, writing in 1940,
argued that Watson's name was not likely to be found on the roster of
the twenty-eight foremost American orators.[14] His early essay observed
that orators like Tom Watson were properly classified as "members of the
lunatic fringe" that fought a foolhardy battle against the entrenched and
powerful industrial capitalism of a new age. In spite of Gunderson's
effort to deal with the "often ignored calamity howlers," his critique did
not deal with Watson specifically and only superficially with the colorful-
ness of the Populist movement.

Gunderson's approach to the rhetoric of the Populist movement established the trend of later works. In a standard textbook treatment of
agrarian rhetoric in the late nineteenth century, Donald H. Ecroyd plotted
the rhetorical problem faced by Populist orators during this period.[15] The
difficulty was how to persuasively bring together isolated and typically
independent-minded farmers. Ecroyd's assessment of the political and
economic background that threatened farmers in the 1880s was well developed. It was not clear, however, why the western region of the country
was singled out for special consideration. Tom Watson was only briefly
mentioned in comparison with Mary Elizabeth Lease of Kansas and her
rhetorical solutions to the particular problems facing Midwestern farmers.

In a 1980 essay entitled, "The One-Gallus Uprising: Southern Discon-
tent," Robert W. Smith focused specifically on the economic plight of the
Southern farmers.[16] He identified the economic and social causes for
agrarian discontent from a broader historical framework than did Ecroyd.
Although Smith began his essay with a long quotation from a Tom
Watson speech and made several references to Watson's rhetoric, no

---

[14]Robert G. Gunderson, "The Calamity Howlers," *Quarterly Journal of Speech* 26
(October 1940): 403.

[15]Donald H. Ecroyd, "The Agrarian Protest," in *America in Controversy: History
of American Public Address,* ed. Holland, 171-84.

[16]Robert W. Smith, "The One-Gallus Uprising: Southern Discontent," in *The
Rhetoric of Protest and Reform: 1878-1898,* ed. Boase, 153-81.

systematic effort was made to critique his discourse.[17] Smith placed Watson in a pivotal role in the Southern Populist movement, but he also devoted much of his effort to an outline of the broad sweep of agrarian arguments unique to the South.

Disturbed with the way most rhetorical scholars considered the Populist movement, Howard S. Erlich reassessed the topic in a 1977 essay.[18] His major concern was how Populist rhetoric had been improperly characterized as "paradoxical, containing at once features which, though contradictory, coexist."[19] In his reassessment, Erlich recommended that Tom Watson's role in formulating the People's Party policy toward the Negro in the South be more closely studied. While this position is well argued by Erlich, he missed the opportunity to expand his paradox theme in Watson's case by considering how the Populist leader changed his position on racial equality later in his life. Erlich did properly recognize the rhetorical complexity of the Populist leaders, but his essay ultimately failed to examine the many paradoxes evident in the early discourse of Tom Watson.

The only published essay by a rhetorical critic dealing specifically with Tom Watson's oratorical career is by G. Jack Gravlee.[20] He made it clear in his introductory observations that Watson should be viewed as a most intricate personality. After noting the long and varied political experience of Watson, Gravlee argued that he had "at least two divergent rhetorical careers."[21] This sensitive assessment of Watson, however, was hampered by the decision to focus primarily on the Georgian's 1904 campaign for the presidency. Gravlee's analysis seemed comprehensive for this specific election, but the essay delivered a very narrow interpretation of Watson's "first rhetorical career." Since the critique appeared in a volume devoted to the study of "Southern Demagogues," most of Gravlee's evidence on Watson's 1904 campaign demonstrated how extreme the Populist had become by this date. Although some biographical information on the Georgian's rhetorical transformation after the critical 1896

---

[17]Ibid., 153-64.

[18]Howard S. Erlich, "Populist Rhetoric Reassessed: A Paradox," *Quarterly Journal of Speech* 63 (April 1977): 140-51.

[19]Ibid., 150.

[20]G. Jack Gravlee, "Tom Watson: Disciple of 'Jeffersonian Democracy'," in *The Oratory of Southern Demagogues,* ed. Logue and Dorgan, 85-108.

[21]Ibid., 86.

election is included, this presentation seems unfair. There can be no doubt that a deeply embittered Tom Watson became a scapegoat-hunting demagogue late in his life, but to attach this label on him too early in his first rhetorical career pigeonholes and greatly oversimplifies the man.

A review of the unpublished doctoral dissertations completed in the fields of American history and speech communication reveals that no writers have treated Watson's rhetoric in the 1880s from the metaphorical perspective of this study. The only related historical work is the 1963 unpublished study by Ted Carageorge comparing the reform strategies of Hoke Smith and Tom Watson.[22] Although Carageorge's primary focus was to evaluate the political strategies of these two local politicians during the 1880s and 1890s, he did provide some careful analysis of Watson's individual speeches. Since Hoke Smith was himself a follower of Henry Grady's New South Creed in the 1880s, Carageorge's critique centered on how Smith effectively used this mythology to fight off the third-party efforts of Watson in the 1890s.

In regard to Henry Woodfin Grady, scholars in the field of speech communication have often debated his relative greatness as a speaker. Charles F. Lindsley was the first to argue Grady's prowess on the stump in a 1920 essay.[23] Even though this early article reflected a simplistic Neo-Aristotelian perspective on Grady's rhetoric, Lindsley did attend to the Georgian's special emphasis on metaphor in the construction of a visual image for his audience. The only major problem with Lindsley's critique was his insistent hyperbole in reviewing the achievements of Grady's oratorical career.

After producing a doctoral dissertation on Grady's speaking career, Marvin G. Bauer condensed his basic conclusions in a 1943 textbook.[24] Bauer believed that Grady was not one of America's "great thinkers," but was instead a "great personality" whose oratorical contributions were cut short by his untimely death. Besides presenting a well-documented outline of Grady's speech training, Bauer observed how potent the "New South" metaphors were for Southerners of the era. Bauer dealt with a

[22]Ted Carageorge, "An Evaluation of Hoke Smith and Thomas E. Watson as Georgia Reformers" (Unpublished doctoral dissertation, University of Georgia, 1963).
[23]Lindsley, 28-42.
[24]Marvin W. Bauer, "Henry Grady," in Vol. 1 of *A History and Criticism of American Public Address*, ed. Brigance, 387-406.

greater variety of Grady's speeches than did Lindsley and provided an excellent bibliography.

In recent years, a number of rhetorical critics have considered Henry Grady's proper role in the history of Southern oratory. David L. Metheny, for example, has analyzed Grady's New South speech from an Hegelian dialectical perspective.[25] He concluded that Grady's speeches were effective because they articulated a romantic vision of nationalism that was dialectically appropriate for the times. Metheny's close analysis of the New South speech was provocative, but he did not apply the Hegelian theory to Grady's other speeches of this crucial era.

The most comprehensive treatment of Grady's oratory yet to appear in the field of speech communication is by Harold D. Mixon.[26] In his fine essay, Mixon has identified three basic themes developed by Grady through most of his major speeches: 1)Economic diversification, 2) Race relations, and 3) Nationalism. Mixon's critique considers how Grady's rhetoric helped propel various mythic images throughout the South in the 1880s. This book will consider some of Mixon's findings in its later analysis.

While most speech communication researchers concede Grady's significant role in formalizing and articulating the progressive New South theme in the 1880s, two writers have recently challenged this perspective. E. Culpepper Clark, for example, has asserted that Francis Warrington Dawson, a rival Southern newspaper editor, deserved as much credit as Grady in symbolically creating the New South Creed.[27] Following a similar line of argument, Louis Campbell has also argued that the orator Walter Hines Page should be seen as a much more pragmatic spokesman for the South during the 1880s.[28] Since both Clark and Campbell suggest potential flaws in the rhetorical stance taken by Grady during this troubled period in Southern history, their assessments will be included within an evaluation of Grady's debate with Watson.

---

[25]David L. Metheny, "The New South: Grady's Use of Hegelian Dialectic," *Southern Speech Journal* 31 (Fall 1965): 34-41.

[26]Harold D. Mixon, "Henry Grady as a Persuasive Strategist," in *Oratory in the New South,* ed. Braden, 74-116.

[27]E. Culpepper Clark, "Henry Grady's New South: A Rebuttal from Charleston," *Southern Speech Communication Journal* 41 (Summer 1976): 346-58.

[28]J. Louis Campbell, "In Search of the New South," *Southern Speech Communication Journal* 47 (Summer 1982): 361-88.

In the field of history, Paul Gaston's *The New South Creed: A Study in Southern Mythmaking*[29] stands as a most insightful analysis of the mythic power of Grady's persuasive efforts in the 1880s and 1890s. The major strength of the work is Gaston's careful tracing of the "manipulation" and slow transformation of Henry Grady's basic premise after the young editor died suddenly in 1889. Although Gaston does not contrast Watson's efforts with those of Grady, Gaston does contend that the New South myth was an important symbolic foil used to put down such political efforts as Southern Populism.[30] Gaston focused on the twentieth-century ramifications of Grady's mythic creed rather than providing a close rhetorical critique of the Georgian's speeches.

Some good biographies of Watson and Grady have been published, but they have to be used with great care. William W. Brewton's *The Life of Thomas E. Watson*,[31] for example, was written while Watson was still alive and with his assistance. This particular work is useful primarily for its long quotations and, sometimes, complete passages from Watson's speeches. Since Brewton was an acknowledged follower of Watson's particular brand of Populism, many of the conclusions drawn from this work will have to be carefully considered for bias.

By comparison to Brewton's volume, C. Vann Woodward's *Tom Watson: Agrarian Rebel* is almost flawless. This work stands as a classic for biographies of its type and will be heavily consulted for its insights into the "early" Tom Watson of the 1880s. Woodward's overall assessment of Watson is exceptional. As a historian, however, Woodward has tended to overlook many of Watson's contributions to Southern oratory.

At present, two complete book-length biographies on the life of Henry W. Grady are available.[32] Raymond B. Nixon's *Henry Grady: Spokesman of the New South* is particularly insightful in its review of Grady's speechmaking throughout the South. While the volume is strong as an extensive chronology of Grady's life, Mills Lane has cautioned that

---

[29]Gaston, *The New South Creed,* 221-22.

[30]Ibid., 222.

[31]William W. Brewton, *The Life of Thomas E. Watson* (Atlanta: The Author, 1926).

[32]Raymond B. Nixon, *Henry W. Grady: Spokesman for the New South* (New York: Alfred A. Knopf, 1943). See also, Davis.

since Nixon wrote this work during wartime, the conclusions must be used with an understanding of its clearly "patriotic" fervor.[33]

The most recent work on Grady in the field of American history is by Harold E. Davis. Though it too has its limitations, Davis's study remains invaluable. Writing in *Henry Grady's New South: Atlanta, A Brave and Beautiful City*, Davis contends that Grady's "heart belonged to Atlanta, not to his region."[34] Using a most impressive variety of primary sources from Grady's personal papers, Davis concludes that "despite what Grady said in his speeches and writings," the editor's "objectives were local and limited" to a grand promotion of Georgia's capital city.[35] Davis also argues that Grady "thought little of ancient languages and liberal studies" and specifically that "speechmakers" were not important in the industrial, business-centered future of the South.[36] In contrast to Davis's perspective, this book will argue that Grady believed his rhetoric to be important for Atlanta and for the entire region and that classical subjects such as rhetoric and oratory were extremely important to Southerners Henry Grady and Tom Watson.

Rationale for the Book

This study will assess the major documents produced by Grady and Watson during the 1880s from a rhetorical perspective focusing on mythic images and metaphors as opposed to the sociological or cultural perspective traditionally applied to these orators. Because of their key role in articulating a new cultural truth for Southerners, the speeches and public editorials of Watson and Grady between 1880 and 1890 will merit the closest attention in this study. No previous study has directly compared Watson's and Grady's speeches as documents emerging from this rhetorical situation that was so unique and culturally vital to the South.

Clement Eaton argues that the antebellum South developed a distinct love and respect for the "power of the spoken (not written) word."[37]

---

[33]Lane, *The New South*, xvi.
[34]Harold E. Davis, *Henry Grady's New South: Atlanta, A Brave and Beautiful City* (Tuscaloosa: University of Alabama Press, 1990) 197.
[35]Ibid., 195.
[36]Ibid., 188.
[37]Clement Eaton, *The Growth of Southern Civilization* (New York: Harper and Row, 1961) 277.

There is much in the oral tradition in the 1880s to suggest that cultural influence over a Southerner's mind continued to depend upon oral communication. W. J. Cash has observed that throughout the South:

> rhetoric flourished far beyond even its American average; it early became a passion—and not only a passion but a primary standard of judgement, the *sine qua non* of leadership. The greatest man would be the man who could best wield it.[38]

The destruction of the economic and social structure in the South after 1865 provided a new demand for direction and leadership that Grady and Watson tried to fulfill rhetorically. As they had so often in their past, Southerners listened hopefully to the competing notions of what to do about their future. Military Reconstruction left most Southerners in need of new ways to talk about the South, in need of dialogue about the future of the South. Grady and Watson provided the dialogue and futuristic vision necessary.

Watson's and Grady's speeches provide important historical evidence of their sentiments on government, politics, and race relations. This study, however, will offer an analysis of Watson's and Grady's public rhetoric in the 1880s as a method to enhance our understanding of the competing images being offered for acceptance during this period. In addition, this metaphorical critique of Watson's and Grady's oratory will help us better understand the theory and power of rhetoric in the South during the later decades of the nineteenth century.

This Study of Grady and Watson

The critical perspective of this volume is metaphorical, viewing Grady's and Watson's speeches of the 1880s as a pervasive symbolic act within the oral tradition of the South. Grady and Watson used metaphors in their speeches to establish a new symbolic vision of the South in the minds of their audience. *Atlanta Constitution* assistant editor Joel Chandler Harris, for example, argued that Henry Grady developed early in his speaking career the use of vivid metaphors that could carry an audience with him

---

[38]W. J. Cash, *The Mind of the South* (New York: Vintage Books, 1969) 53.

in a speech.[39] Watson also possessed a keen interest in the identifying power of metaphor. C. Vann Woodward observes that Watson had "a certain talent for robust metaphor and gargantuan simile struck off with spontaneity in the genuine rural idiom."[40] From these accounts, it is clear that an understanding of Watson's and Grady's oratory requires a very close examination of their metaphors.

The importance of metaphorical analysis for this period of Southern history has not been completely ignored by scholars. Bruce Palmer, a historian who has closely examined the Southern Populist movement of the 1890s, argues that the Southern orator of this turbulent period must be understood "through their inherited ways of understanding the world around them—the producerite, Jeffersonian-Jacksonian, religious and moral metaphors and images" of the time.[41]

Critical Perspective of the Book

Since the time of Aristotle, rhetoricians have pondered the cultural implications of metaphor in language. Aristotle observed in his *Poetics* that the "greatest thing by far" in the use of language "is to be the master of metaphor."[42] He defined this as an art which "implies an intuitive perception of the similarity in dissimilars." In the Aristotelian perspective, the use of metaphor was not something that could be learned but was a "true sign of genius." As an intuitive gift developed only by those artistically inclined, metaphor would be commanded, in Aristotle's view, only by the best speakers and writers.

This method of metaphorical analysis will not assess the type or variety of "ornaments" speakers add to language; instead, it will view metaphors in the romantic perspective as opposed to the classical position of Aristotle, first advanced by the Italian rhetorician Giambattista Vico.[43] Writing in 1725, Vico argued in his *New Science* that "general metaphor

---

[39]Joel Chandler Harris, ed. *Life of Henry W. Grady* (New York: Cassell Publishing, 1890) 70.

[40]Woodward, *Tom Watson*, 47-48.

[41]Bruce Palmer, *Man Over Money: The Southern Populist Critique of American Capitalism* (Chapel Hill: University of North Carolina Press, 1980) 219-20.

[42]Ingram Bywater, trans. *The Poetic of Aristotle* (New York: Modern Library, 1954) 255.

[43]Terrence Hawkes, *Metaphor* (London: Methuen, 1972) 38.

makes up the great body of the language among all nations."[44] Through this common language, Vico observed, cultures maintain their creative and cohesive structure. He further contended that:

> There must be in the nature of human institutions a mental language common to all nations which uniformly grasps the substance of things feasible in human social life and expresses it with as many diverse modifications as these same things have diverse aspects.[45]

Isaiah Berlin has commented on the theory's appropriateness for studying the influence of rhetoric on history. Vico envisioned a study of metaphors in language that would reveal the "history of things signified by words," Berlin contends that historians or rhetoricians possess the rhetorical key by which to comprehend how meanings of words change or are modified mentally in the successive phases of a civilization.[46] Berlin concludes that a rhetorician could reconstruct a dictionary of the basic mental language or ideas common to people in a given culture. Such central ideas to be considered would be: *gods, family, authority, conquest, sacrifices, rights, command, courage,* and *fame.* These terms or metaphorical references to them, notes Berlin, are the basic forms or ideas which all human beings must have conceived of and lived by at some time or another in their history.[47]

Strongly influenced by Vico's *New Science,* I. A. Richards's *Philosophy of Rhetoric* asserts metaphor as the "omnipresent principle" of all language.[48] Richards advises critics of rhetoric that a study of metaphor would allow an insight into how new meanings are symbolically constructed in the mind of an audience. Richards argues that effective rhetorical criticism would reveal that "thought is metaphoric and proceeds by comparison."[49]

---

[44]Thomas G. Bergin and Max H. Fisch, *The New Science of Giambattista Vico* (Ithaca: Cornell University Press, 1970) 104.

[45]Ibid., 25.

[46]Isaiah Berlin, *Vico and Herder: Two Studies in the History of Ideas* (New York: Viking Press, 1976) 47.

[47]Ibid., 48-49.

[48]I. A. Richards, *The Philosophy of Rhetoric* (London: Oxford University Press, 1936) 90.

[49]Ibid., 94.

As an advocate of the "romantic" view of metaphor presented by Vico, Richards specifically disagrees with the Aristotelian position in three ways. First, Richards denies that use of metaphor is a special gift for a select few in a society. He contends that through special "teaching and study," most people will come to command this pervasive dimension of language. Second, Richards points out that the use of metaphor develops through the general process of using language and thus the learning is part of the characteristics that make us "distinctively human." Finally, Richards argues that metaphors are not the exception in the common use of language. Instead, metaphor is placed as central in the normal use of language and is, therefore, "the omnipresent principle of all free action."[50]

After refuting Aristotle's position on metaphor, Richards outlines his own perspective on this central feature of language. He defines metaphor as the "use of one reference to a group of things that are related in a particular way in order to discover a similar relation in another group."[51] In Richards's theory, individuals attribute meaning by simply seeing in one context an aspect similar to that encountered in another context. As a process of mental transference, two thoughts of different things are supported by a single word or phrase and derive meaning from their interaction.

In his advice to literary critics, Richards explains how metaphors can best be analyzed from the perspective of potential readers. Since metaphor is the means by which meaning is developed, it is also the process by which a rhetor may provide his audience with the experience needed to elicit similar references for a particular word or phrase.[52] As a key to experience and meanings, Richards observes that the speaker or writer often seeks to "supply and control a large part of the listener's experience." In this way, the rhetor can assert a sense of control and modification over the audience's interpretation of experience.

Following from the theory of metaphor he proposes, Richards advises critics to consider metaphor as a mental combination of tenor and vehicle. Tenor is the term referring to the underlying idea or principle subject of the metaphor. Vehicle is the means of conveying the underlying idea,

---

[50]Ibid., 92.

[51]I. A. Richards and C. K. Ogden, *The Meaning of Meaning* (New York: Harcourt Brace, 1930) 213.

[52]Sonja K. Foss, Karen A. Foss, and Robert A. Trapp, *Contemporary Perspectives on Rhetoric* (Prospect Heights, Illinois: Waveland Press, 1985) 33-34.

the borrowed idea, or what the tenor resembles. These terms taken together also define similarity as an important feature of metaphor. While
Richards urges literary critics to examine closely how tenor and vehicle
interact within a text, he also argues that metaphors presented in an oral
context may be best critiqued by focusing on the level of disparity or
dissimilarity.[53] Considering Richards's recommendations, this study will
primarily consider specific references in Grady's and Watson's metaphors
by the level of disparity and dissimilarity they contain.

Richards's theory for the textual analysis of metaphors has its limitations. While Richards briefly mentions culture in his works, he views this
social interaction as a very sterile or "scientific" environment. Max
Black, in an extension and critique of Richards's theory, has noted that
the *Philosophy of Rhetoric* offers few details as to how the "meanings"
of words are modified by their contexts, how word order is significant,
and how metaphors may address the wider symbolic environment of
cultural interaction.[54] In his specific recommendations for critics, Black
urges that special attention be given to how writers or speakers use
references in their environment to fashion "associated commonplaces"
between themselves and various audiences. These commonplaces,
contends Black, are mentally modified in the process of interaction
between speaker or writer by "associated implications" inherent in the use
of metaphor.[55] Since these new implications should forge a new interpretation from the constant oral or written interaction of a rhetor, Black
advises rhetorical critics to carefully study the common ground evident
or implied between a rhetor and audience. This volume, therefore, will
pay special attention to those social and cultural commonplaces asserted
by Grady and Watson between themselves and their Southern audience.

Following the perspectives of metaphor provided by Vico, Richards,
Berlin, and Black, this analysis will reveal the important elements of
Southern thought held by Southerners as to their region's future. The
identification of Watson's and Grady's metaphors, therefore, will allow
the reconstruction of the new mental vision that both orators attempted

---

[53]I. A. Richards, *Interpretations in Teaching* (New York: Harcourt Brace, 1938)
133.

[54]Max Black, *Language and Philosophy* (Ithaca: Cornell University Press, 1944)
206-15.

[55]Max Black, *Models and Metaphors* (Ithaca: Cornell University Press, 1962) 44-
45.

to transfer to their audiences at a time when the South was entering a new phase of civilization. This metaphorical critique may offer new theoretical insights into how metaphors can shape the collective consciousness of an entire geographic region.

Contributions and Limitations

It is important at the beginning to make clear the several limitations of this study. The hundreds of rhetorical documents produced by Grady and Watson during their lifetimes are doubtlessly subject to a variety of critical interpretations beyond the scope of this study. No effort is made here to present a comprehensive biographical treatment either of Watson or Grady, even for the period under investigation (approximately 1880 to 1889). The events, persons, and ideas selected for discussion are limited to those which seem to have most influenced Grady and Watson to metaphorically generate a comprehensive vision for the future economic and social life of the typical white Southerner. This limitation may be most telling in the decision to omit a discussion of political rhetoric. Watson and Grady were intimately involved throughout the period with Georgia and even national Democratic politics. Except where necessary, political references will be avoided in favor of a consideration of Watson's and Grady's influence on the intellectual, social, and cultural developments in the South.

Finally, this study is not intended as a test case for the exercise of metaphorical criticism; the merits of such studies have been amply demonstrated in several published studies in recent years.[56] As one of the few rhetorical critics considering the importance of metaphors, Michael Osborn has specifically adapted the metaphorical philosophy of Vico and Richards within a unique framework.[57] In the practice of analyzing metaphor in public address, Osborn advised that they always occupy important positions with the most significant speeches of a society. Osborn argues that metaphors should be found at the most critical junctures in a speech:

---

[56]See, for example, Michael Osborn, "Archetypal Metaphor in Rhetoric: The Light-Dark Family," *Quarterly Journal of Speech* 53 (April 1967): 115-26 and Herman G. Stelzner, "Ford's War on Inflation: A Metaphor that Did not Cross," *Communication Monographs* 44 (November 1977): 284-97.

[57]Michael Osborn and Douglas Ehninger, "The Metaphor in Public Address," *Speech Monographs* 24 (August 1962): 223-34.

establishing a mood and perspective in the introduction, reinforcing a critical argument in the body, and synthesizing the meaning and force of a speech at its conclusion.[58] Because of metaphors' persuasive power, Osborn concludes that speeches concerned with changing society or directed at audiences beyond the immediate setting are often filled with metaphorical imagery. Since both Grady's and Watson's discourse contained metaphors at crucial junctures and were concerned with change in Southern society, Osborn's recommendations will help guide this study's analysis of their metaphors.[59]

Students of Southern public address have typically emphasized the role played by Grady's and Watson's oratory in reflecting or acting upon larger social and ideological concerns. While this perspective is certainly legitimate and will not be neglected by this present study, these concerns tend to reduce the significance of rhetorical action as a primary factor that shapes and determines human endeavor. Since both Watson and Grady were intimately concerned with the creation of the most fitting and proper rhetorical act, their discourse represents an instance of rhetorical action speaking most directly to the human communicative, rather than political or economic nature. Grady's and Watson's rhetoric, therefore, illustrates that communication plays a vital socializing and intellectually motivating role, rather than merely reflecting the course of human affairs.[60] Rhetorical scholars should make the case for the ways in which human symbolic interaction shapes the questions and answers of history. To that larger project, this study is meant to contribute in small part.

---

[58]Michael Osborn, "Archetypal Metaphor in Rhetoric: The Light-Dark Family," 116-17.

[59]For an in-depth comparison of Osborn's approach and Vico's perspective, see Ferald J. Bryan "Vico on Metaphor: Implications for Rhetorical Criticism," *Philosophy and Rhetoric* 19 (1986): 255-65.

[60]For a summary of Grady's contributions to Southern public address, see Ferald J. Bryan, "Henry Grady, Southern Statesman," in *American Orators Before 1900: Critical Studies and Sources*, ed. Duffy and Ryan, 197-204.

Chapter 1

The Southern
Mind and Metaphor

"A manner of speaking, an accent, a quality of voice, common in a
large measure to all Southerners regardless of race, creed, or color are
the most widely possessed and most obvious characteristics of Southerners."

—Henry Savage
Seeds of Time

"Tell about the South. What's it like there? What do they do there?
Why do they live there? Why do they live at all?"

—William Faulkner
Absalom, Absalom!

Southerners of all races and classes confronted a harsh winter of great
decisions at the end of Federal Reconstruction. When President Rutherford B. Hayes formally removed Federal troops from the Statehouses of
Louisiana and South Carolina in 1877, most "Carpetbag" regimes in the
rural South promptly collapsed.[1] White Democratic Southerners slowly
regained control of their political destiny by the end of the 1870s, but the
economic and social consequences of the Civil War and Reconstruction
continued to affect the South well into the turn of the century. Bewilder-
ed by the destruction and decay of their traditional way of life, the Southern people sought out spokesmen to explain the events of their past and
to guide them toward a more prosperous future.

This chapter will explore the diversity of the rhetorical legacy and
common symbolic associations that influenced the Southern audience of
the 1880s. First, it will outline the economic traditions of the Southern

---

[1]C. Vann Woodward, *Origins of the New South: 1877-1913* (Baton Rouge:
Louisiana State University Press, 1951) 45.

farmer before and after the war. Next, it will examine the power and
symbolism of blending religious and economic metaphors for the rural
Southern audience. Finally, it will discuss the emergence of Henry Grady
and Tom Watson within the Southern rhetorical tradition.

The Southern Mind and Agriculture

The legacy of the Civil War on Southern farmers was particularly harsh.
Before the war, the large planter aristocracy dominated Southern agriculture. These wealthy farmers lost not only their fortunes in Confederate
securities, but their land was virtually worthless since they lacked the
means to work it.[2] Without machinery, seed, and a dependable supply of
labor, thousands of acres of the best Southern farmland were sold for
three to five dollars an acre. Many thousands of acres were simply abandoned by their owners. Grand homes, barns, fences, and railroads
throughout the South lay in complete ruin.[3] Since the Union Army under
the direction of General William T. Sherman decided to single out the
people of the Georgia countryside for a "scorched earth" treatment, farmers in that state were in especially difficult positions.

In Georgia, as in other Southern states, the demise of the large planter aristocracy meant that the small farmers soon came to predominate
agriculture in the South; however, they rarely had the resources to actually own the land they worked. With the extreme shortage of currency,
they were forced into an extensive system of credit and tenant farming.
Alex Mathews Arnett argues that perhaps as many as eighty to ninety
percent of the cotton growers in Georgia participated in the crop-lien
system.[4]

Under the crop-lien system, a farmer would sign a written contract
with a landlord or merchant requiring that in exchange for advance use
of "horses, mules, oxen, necessary provisions, farming tools and imple-
ments or money to purchase the same," the contracting farmer would sign
over, as a guarantee that the account would be paid, his "entire crop of

[2]John D. Hicks, *The Populist Revolt* (Lincoln: University of Nebraska Press, 1961)
37.

[3]Hicks, 37.

[4]Alex Mathews Arnett, *The Populist Movement in Georgia* (New York: Longmans,
Green and Co., 1920) 57. See also Barton C. Shaw, *The Wool-Hat Boys: Georgia's
Populist Party* (Baton Rouge: Louisiana State University Press, 1984) 14-15.

cotton, cotton-seed, corn, fodder, peas, and potatoes."[5] This contract frequently required the farmer to put up his personal property and chattels as part of this special mortgage. If, at the end of the harvest season, the farmer was unable to pay his entire indebtedness out of the proceeds of the season's crop, he was legally obligated, by the original crop-lien contract, to continue trading with the merchant or landlord who held the lien until the account could be settled in full.[6]

The crop-lien system, as it evolved in the 1880s, became a great "pawnshop" for the farmers caught up in it. As Arnett has observed, the Georgia farmer's account was rarely ever "settled in full," instead, "when a crop was harvested, it did not belong to the farmer; it must go at once to the merchant."[7] Under these conditions, the farmer could not hold out his crop for a better price, nor seek a more advantageous season. The farmer was trapped in passive submission to the landlord or merchant because the harvest rarely provided enough money to pay his ever-increasing debt.[8]

The high cost of the items purchased on credit and the declining market value of cotton created larger and larger debts for tenant farmers. Because the farmer had to depend on the services of his local furnishing merchant, he could not shop around for better rates on the goods he had to buy in order to get his crop in the ground. Typically, the farmer paid from twenty to fifty percent more for what he bought on credit than he would have paid if he had been able to buy for cash.[9] If this were not enough of a hardship, the average market price for cotton declined from 9.5 cents per pound in 1881 to 7.8 cents per pound by the end of the decade.[10] The results of the high credit prices of the crop-lien system and the falling prices of cotton meant that most Southern farmers endured the 1880s in poverty. In 1890, the per capita income of Southerners was only fifty-one percent of the national average.[11]

Even as the economic gloom of the 1880s darkened for most farmers, there was little that they could look forward to in terms of personal

---

[5]Hicks, 43.
[6]Hicks, 43.
[7]Arnett, 57.
[8]Arnett, 75.
[9]Hicks, 44; See also Shaw, 14.
[10]Hicks, 55-56.
[11]Carl N. Degler, *Place Over Time: The Continuity of Southern Distinctiveness* (Baton Rouge: Louisiana State University Press, 1977) 118.

betterment. As a direct result of the poor economic base throughout the South, public education was a major causality. During the decade, the average length of the common school term in the South fell off approximately twenty percent.[12] In addition, the amount of money expended per capita of student population declined throughout the region. In 1890, the per capita expenditure on Southern students was ninety-seven cents, as compared with $2.24 in the nation as a whole.[13]

In the state of Georgia, the educational system lagged even further behind the developments in the North. For the small farmers, education of their children depended on the quality of old field schools. Often located on unused cotton fields, these schools were local community enterprises; local people built the school house, hired the teacher, furnished the children, and paid the bills.[14] Most poor Georgia children in the rural areas enrolled in these schools for an average desultory attendance of two to three years.

For the majority of Southerners, both before and after the war, agriculture was typically associated with symbolic conceptions of the "good life." The experience of life was often interpreted through metaphoric prisms of preserving the past in memories and expecting the future to be very similar in its economic requirements. With traditional antebellum farm life destroyed forever by the war and the economy worsening through the early 1880s, the symbolic universe for Southerners lacked hope and purpose. The first rhetorical vision that offered any comfort was the familiar associations and heavenly control found in religious metaphors.

Southern Religious Rhetoric
And Economic Recovery

Without good prospects for personal advancement in this life, downtrodden Southerners clung to the idea of the better life promised in the hereafter. Religion played a critical role in the thinking of the Southerner about his future as he contemplated the new decade of the 1880s, and it

---

[12]Woodward, *Origins of the New South*, 61-62.

[13]Ibid., 62-63.

[14]Numan V. Bartley, *The Creation of Modern Georgia* (Athens: University of Georgia Press, 1983) 26-27.

was through religious metaphors that the new rhetorical leaders appealed to the Southern masses.

While the economic interests of the Southern gentry and yeomentry were not the same before the Civil War, each class depended on the symbolic security of the cotton kingdom. The Southern preacher, pressured by both classes, helped to maintain political solidarity and even sanctioned the cause of slavery as a unique and necessary economic enterprise. Before the war, Southern religious theology was symbolically modified to fit the particular situation faced by the slave-holding region.

Southern Baptists, Presbyterians, Methodists, and other major denominations separated from their Northern counterparts over the issue of slavery.[15] As the Abolition movement gained momentum through the moral arguments against slavery by such forceful spokesmen as William Lloyd Garrison and Theodore Dwight Weld, Southern ministers typically argued the case for slavery as part of their regular Sunday sermons.

Starting in the early 1800s, Southern preachers marshalled a variety of arguments in defense of slavery. In the 1820s, for example, Dr. Richard Furman, a Baptist minister in South Carolina, argued the support of slavery on moral grounds. He insisted that a race bound by "ignorance and error" could not be free and true liberty consisted not in name but in reality.[16] As an extension of this position, Thomas R. Dew, a professor at William and Mary College, contended on the eve of the Civil War that the institution of slavery was as old as the human race and had been held in honor even among the Jews. Further, he pointed out that slavery was beneficial to the world because it reduced the number of wars by introducing ignorant slaves to cultured society, in which they might be trained for productive labor and enjoy a standard of living higher than they could have attained in their former habitat.[17] In conclusion, Dew noted that slavery helped elevate Southern society by upgrading the status of women and generally fostering a deeper sense of equality among whites through the assignment of the Negro to all menial tasks. Dew's position, in effect, summarized the classical Greek notion of democracy that visualized a

---

[15]Hubert Vance Taylor, "Preaching on Slavery," in *Preaching in American History,* ed. Holland, 169-70.

[16]Clifton E. Olmstead, *History of Religion in the United States* (Englewood Cliffs, New Jersey: Prentice-Hall, 1960) 373.

[17]Olmstead, 374.

citizenry devoted to government and education, freed from the necessity of physical labor.

As a rationalization of an institution subject to the attack of the abolitionists, Southerners turned to orators like John C. Calhoun, William A. White, and Alexander Stephens who argued the existence of a "Great Chain of Being" in Southern society. The white man, as the only fit race, was to occupy one of the topmost links of the cultural chain. The Negro, as God and Nature ordained, being of an inferior order of being, was to be kept in a complete state of subjection, not only for the good of the Southern planters, but for his own good, and for the good of society as well.[18]

Combined with the cultural rationalization for slavery and the moral justification for assisting an inferior being, Southern preachers turned the Civil War into a "glorious religious crusade."[19] The Reverend Henry H. Tucker, speaking before the Georgia Legislature on November 15, 1861, exclaimed that "it is important for us to remember,—that GOD is in the War. He brought it among us!"[20] While Northern ministers cited slavery as a sin unique to the South, preachers in Virginia and Georgia responded by citing Northern materialism as a sin and as the leading cause for God's wrath. The Reverend Thomas V. Moore of Richmond, Virginia said that "a long course of peace and prosperity, acting on our depraved nature tends to emasculate and corrupt a people."[21] Ministers like Moore reasoned that the unprecedented prosperity of the United States had corrupted the whole nation to the point where God was forced to act by bringing sectional war. These Southern preachers, however, believed that the agricultural South had been much less guilty of materialism and moral corruption than had the highly industrialized North.[22] Wealthy Southern planters may have quarreled with the materialism metaphor, but they were nevertheless part of the unified rhetorical vision that led to war.

---

[18]Anthony Hillbrunner, "Inequality, the Great Chain of Being, and Antebellum Southern Oratory," *Southern Speech Journal* 24 (Spring 1960): 188-89.

[19]Charles Stewart, "Civil War Preaching," in *Preaching in American History*, ed. Holland, 188-89.

[20]Stewart, 187.

[21]As cited by Stewart, 188.

[22]Stewart, 188-89.

Even with the belief and encouragement of a heavenly sanction, Southerners of all classes were forced to accept the verdict of Appomattox. With the antebellum religious vision swept away by Grant's and Sherman's armies, the Southern clergy turned to a new, more positive view of what God had in store for the South. The rural preaching still maintained its frontier revivalism tone with a clear exposition on the joys of heaven and the horrors of hell. In Southern post-Civil War theology, there remained a strong preoccupation with personal salvation—a vision of a fallen individual realizing his sinful state and repenting to an omnipotent God.[23] This tendency for poor rural Southerners to encourage a personal relationship with God is best summarized by W. J. Cash:

What our Southerner required . . . was a faith as simple and emotional as himself. A faith to draw men together in hordes, to terrify them with Apocalyptic rhetoric, to cast them into the pit, rescue them, and at last bring them shouting into the fold of Grace. A faith not of liturgy and prayer book, but of primitive frenzy and the blood sacrifice—often of fits and jerks and barks. The God demanded was an anthropomorphic God—the Jehovah of the Old Testament; a God who might be seen, a God who *had* been seen. A passionate, whimsical tyrant, to be trembled before, but whose favor was the sweeter for that. A personal God, a God for the individualist, a God whose representatives were not silken priests, but preachers risen from the people themselves.[24]

Rising from the destruction of the War, Southern ministers fought rhetorically to provide meaning to life and society amid the baffling failure of the South's holy cause. The harsh lesson of evil triumphing— by God's command—was not an easy thing for the Southern mind, rich or poor, to accept. But, as Charles Reagan Wilson observes, this defeat did not alter the Southerners' self-image: "God's chosen people did not give up that chosen status" even when defeated.[25] Southerners, as they entered the 1880s, retained a strong sense of religious and sectional pride. They came to believe, as their preachers argued, that God would bring good out of triumphant evil. This new destiny would be even greater than

---

[23]Rollin G. Osterweis, *The Myth of the Lost Cause: 1865-1900* (Hamden, Connecticut: Archon Books, 1973) 119.

[24]W. J. Cash, *The Mind of the South* (New York: Vintage Books, 1969) 58.

[25]Charles Reagan Wilson, *Baptized in Blood: The Religion of the Lost Cause 1865-1920* (Athens: University of Georgia Press, 1980) 77.

their pre-Civil War past, and Southerners, as the chosen people, must pre-
pare for their special future. The stress was on the future, the need for
communal solidarity, and the conviction that God would demand great
achievements from Southerners.[26] These positive, almost mystic associations with the Southern past were still apparent to a Southern audience,
but would demand modification for the still undefined future.

Southern Religion, Rhetoric and Metaphor

In order to best understand the development of the diverse aspects of the
Southern audience through its economic and religious turmoil in the late
nineteenth century, one must consider how deeply the antebellum South
respected the practice of rhetoric and dialogue. This art was especially
revered by the gentry, but it filtered down to the lower classes as well.
From its earliest history, the South developed a cult of chivalry modeled
on the classical Greek pattern. With rich plantation owners serving as the
aristocracy, the cult of chivalry became an ideal that determined manners,
military affairs and romantic oratory.[27] In the Old South, ambitious men,
both rich and poor, followed the Greek philosophy that oratory was the
key to power in a democratic society. Every crossroad settlement in the
South developed a debating club for its young gentlemen. In most of the
Southern colleges, roles of honor were earned not on the athletic field but
in the debating societies. Many students in these academic environments
claimed they learned more of permanent value from their speech preparation for these debating forums than they did from their regular class
work.[28]

Richard Weaver, a thoughtful scholar of the Southern rhetorical tradition, has traced the development of this oral process in the South's
intellectual history. In his review of late nineteenth-century Southern
rhetoric, Weaver identified the study of metaphor as critical to understanding Southern thinking during this period. Because social scientists
have ignored the philosophical significance of metaphor in explaining the
actions of Southerners after the Civil War, Weaver concluded that they

---

[26]Wilson, 77-78.

[27]Rollin G. Osterweis, *Romanticism and Nationalism in the Old South* (New
Haven: Yale University Press, 1949) 55.

[28]Osterweis, *Romanticism and Nationalism in the Old South*, 94-95.

failed to understand "that metaphor is itself a means of discovery."[29] Weaver sees metaphor as a "most important heuristic device, leading us from a known to an unknown, but subsequently verifiable, fact or principle."[30]

Weaver's perspective on the relationship between late nineteenth-century rhetoric and metaphor is very much within the tradition established by intellectual historians of this period. For example, Henry Nash Smith has argued that American thought was shaped and influenced during the early part of the nineteenth century by the extremely attractive and emotional metaphor captured in the vision of a "virgin land."[31] Starting from the rhetoric of Thomas Jefferson, a romantic vision, created and extended by metaphors, helped to encourage settlers to leave their "original nests" and take command of the vacant, fertile land located in the American West. The pioneers who ventured west looked to these agrarian metaphors for encouragement to help them take command of the wild American interior and master all of its secrets.[32]

The emotional force of metaphor to fuel romantic visions should not be neglected in the study of Southern history or rhetoric. I. A. Richards has cautioned rhetoricians to remember that it is literal language that is, in fact, rare in the cultural dialogue and that metaphor is central to the study of all discourse. In his view, a comparison of two objects is forced upon the mind in a sudden and striking fashion. The result of this comparison process, argues Richards, is that the mind becomes a connecting organ. Metaphors force comparisons and this generates tension in the mind for a change in thinking. Listeners often tire of comparisons and the tension, but a level of identification between speaker and listener can occur with a new vision created and the distinctions from old to new are drawn particularly sharp.[33] A new viewpoint, a combination of the metaphor and its mental linkages to old or new images in the mind, is thus created.

---

[29]Richard Weaver, *The Ethics of Rhetoric* (South Bend, Indiana: Gateway Editions, 1953) 203.

[30]Ibid., 203.

[31]Henry Nash Smith, *Virgin Land: The American West as Symbol and Myth* (New York: Vintage Books, 1950) 3-11.

[32]Ibid., 12-13.

[33]I. A. Richards, *The Philosophy of Rhetoric* (London: Oxford University Press, 1936) 117-18.

For the late nineteenth-century South, metaphors became the standard by which to follow the development of Southern rhetoric. Weaver contends that any investigation must start from the recognition of certain minimal likenesses then progress through "a series of metaphorical constructs that can be tested as a new cultural truth."[34] As Southern culture developed, rhetoric defined a new vision of truth by giving people "feelings that determined a common attitude toward large phases of experiences."[35] Since Southern rhetors would be particularly attuned to the common metaphors that identified the South's mode of thinking, Weaver notes that these speakers attempted to "create an informed appetition for the Good."[36] Use of these value metaphors would draw a comparison between a commonly accepted good or cultural truth and a new mental construct or association to be accepted. In this metaphoric role, the rhetor serves as a special kind of cultural physician by providing new possibilities for the society in his particular use of metaphors.

When an orator stepped before a Southern audience, the listeners expected any new proposal for the future to be carefully associated with the metaphors of the past that the futuristic notion most closely resembled. In this way, effective rhetors could restructure the symbolic universe of their listeners and could alter their way of thinking about the future.

James Edie explains that metaphors used in broad cultural appeals do much more than just identify possibilities for the people facing uncertainty. Edie states: "The metaphorical use of word thus brings about a reorganization, a refocusing of experience, which continues to grow in complexity with each further use of the word in a distinctly new sense, with each new *purpose*."[37] From Edie's standpoint, the use of a new metaphor provides an important transition in thought, and, by studying metaphors in their historical contexts, scholars can identify these transitions. Since the diverse Southern audience underwent a traumatic shift in its thinking after the Civil War, the metaphors used in the pre-war period would isolate the particular vision common to most Southerners.

---

[34]Weaver, *Ethics of Rhetoric*, 204.

[35]As cited in Sonja K. Foss, Karen A. Foss, and Robert Trapp, *Contemporary Perspectives on Rhetoric* (Prospect Heights, Illinois: Waveland Press, 1985) 52-53.

[36]As cited in Richard L. Johannesen, Rennard Strickland, and Ralph T. Eubanks, eds., *Language is Sermonic: Richard M. Weaver on the Nature of Rhetoric* (Baton Rouge: Louisiana State University Press, 1970) 16-17.

[37]James M. Edie, *Speaking and Meaning* (Bloomington: Indiana University Press, 1976) 188.

Before the war, political rhetors, with morally-charged metaphors, helped to unify all classes of white Southerners to the defense of slavery, the perceived economic base of their existence.

By reviewing the rhetoric of John C. Calhoun and Robert A. Toombs, the importance of metaphorical constructs as a unifying force for Southern audiences becomes clear. As a distinguished United States Senator from South Carolina, Calhoun was especially interested in explaining the proper relationship of the individual states to the federal government. On March 5, 1850, Calhoun delivered his final speech before the United States Senate and stated that the South had the legal and moral right to secede from the Union in defense of slavery. In the Calhoun vision, the Secession cause was justified because the central government had become too autocratic and despotic in nature.

The significant metaphor that emerges from the text of Calhoun's final speech is that of a "shredded fabric." In Calhoun's vision, Northern agitation against slavery was snapping the great "common cords which bound the states together in one Union."[38] The makeup of the cords that held the national fabric together were "spiritual, ecclesiastical, or political in nature," yet, one by one, these strands were breaking.

The first broken cord was that suffered when the Methodist Episcopal church split into Northern and Southern divisions. Calhoun observed that instead of a feeling of "attachment and devotion to the interests of the whole church," the two "hostile bodies" were "engaged in litigation about what was formerly their common property."[39] The strongest religious cord was the Baptist denomination. Calhoun noted that this division was especially significant because the Baptists were "one of the largest and most respectable" of the Protestant denominations.[40] With this portion of the holy national fabric unraveled, Calhoun concluded that only one of the four great Protestant denominations was left "unbroken and entire." In his speech, Calhoun was especially concerned with the common religious traditions that held the national character together.

Calhoun feared the snapping of political cords in the nation as well. The Senator attributed the cause of this political break to Northern agitation and emphasis on force. He pointed out that the use of force was no

---

[38]As cited in A. Craig Baird, *American Public Addresses 1740-1952* (New York: McGraw-Hill, 1956) 80-81.

[39]Baird, 81.

[40]Baird, 81.

match for a political or spiritual Union—a "union of free, independent states, in one confederation, as they stood in the early stages of the Government, and which is only worthy of the sacred name of Union."[41] Calhoun's metaphors provided clues on how to prevent sectional strife. He contended that measures must be adopted that would satisfy the Southern states and be consistent with their sense of "honor and safety." Calhoun took for granted the South's special concept of honor and regional pride. He claimed that the South had always retained the constitutional right to secede from the Union and that all the South wanted was "justice, simple justice and less she ought not to take."[42]

The metaphors inherent in the rhetoric of Calhoun in 1850 suggest a vision just beginning to solidify for most Southerners. Since the spiritual and political reasons that lead the Southern States to join the Union had been snapped by unrelenting Northern agitation, Southerners now had the right to form their own "confederation." The loose confederation-of-states metaphor would later be used to justify the secession of eleven Southern states from the Union by late 1861.

Three years after Calhoun addressed the United States Senate on the slavery question, Georgia Senator Robert Toombs delivered an oration at Emory College in Oxford, Georgia, on the same issue. On this occasion, Toombs employed the same kind of metaphorical image as did Calhoun. He argued that the efforts of "domestic enemies" had "shaken the national government to its deep foundations and bursted the bonds of Christian unity in our land."[43] With this religious metaphor, Toombs indicated his belief in the sinful actions of the Northern agitators against the South.

The major intent, however, of Toombs's speech was to justify and vindicate the "wisdom, humanity, and justice" of the slave system. After citing numerous historical and Biblical examples of the successful enslavement of blacks, Toombs argued:

> I hold . . . that the African is unfit to be intrusted with political power, and incapable as a freeman of securing his own happiness or contributing to the public prosperity, and that whenever the two races co-exist, a state of slavery is best for him and for society. And under it, in our

---

[41]Baird, 82.

[42]Baird, 85.

[43]As cited in Ernest J. Wrage and Barnet Baskerville, *American Forum: Speeches on Historic Issues 1788-1900* (New York: Harper and Brothers, 1960) 159.

country, he is in a better condition than any he has ever attained in any other age and country, either in bondage or freedom.[44]

It is clear that the Senator believed in the Great Chain of Being social order in the South and that this hierarchy must be carefully preserved. In a comparison to the examples in other countries, Toombs noted that

we have not only elevated the African above his own race in any other country, but that his condition is superior to that of millions of laborers in England, who neglects her own to look after the condition of our operatives.[45]

Toombs vigorously defended the specialness of the Southern system. His metaphors suggested the economic, political, and moral superiority of the Southern way of doing things. In particular, he argued that the slave in Georgia, considering his "comforts of life," was paid more than the "free laborer" and certainly treated better than the noblemen of England treated their paid laborers. Toombs concluded by pointing out how the American laborer in the North suffered from a special kind of slavery. He said:

Each individual laborer of the North is the victim not only of his folly and extravagance, but of ignorance, misfortune, and necessities. His isolation enlarges his expenses without increasing his comforts, his want of capital increases the price of everything he buys, disables him from supplying his wants at favorable times, or advantageous terms, and throws him in the hand of retailers and extortioners.[46]

Toombs's metaphors reveal his vision of a crushing, dehumanizing, and exploitative system used by the North that was far worse than the slave system of the South. The Southerner was only doing his Christian and natural duty to maintain the "unified system of labor and capital" that the slavery system represented. On the other hand, the Northern economic leaders were attempting to form an "unholy, unnatural alliance" with politicians that would abolish slavery. The result of this action, noted Toombs, would be a "divided and destroyed" nation.

---

[44]Wrage and Baskerville, 161.
[45]Wrage and Baskerville, 163.
[46]Wrage and Baskerville, 167.

Influenced by the metaphorical imagery in the rhetoric of respected speakers such as Calhoun and Toombs, Southerners united to defend their way of life as they perceived it on the eve of the volleys at Fort Sumter. Even after the war, there was still some sense of cohesion, but a different rhetoric containing different metaphors was required to bring order to the economically and socially confused Southern audience. Orators in the post-war era could present new metaphors to outline the uncertain future, but these new metaphors would have to contain rhetorical bridges connecting them to the still very real past images of slavery, plantations, and a simple social hierarchy.

Religious rhetors made the first effort to provide a sense of social order and economic certainty after the surrender at Appomattox. During the 1870s, Southern ministers spoke out against the invasion of Northern economic culture. Even though Southern farmers and the South's economy in general needed immediate financial attention, the clergy warned against any rapid economic change. As Calhoun and Toombs indicated before the war, the South had long prided itself on self-sufficiency in most economic matters.

The end of the Reconstruction era meant that the Southern economy had to change, and Southern ministers feared new sinful temptations for their congregations. One Nashville religious journal threatened its readers with the likelihood of new sins inherent in adopting the Northern model of industrial development. The Nashville *Advocate* argued:

> When mammonism thus possesses the people they soon become prepared to make almost any concession of moral principle to the demands of commercial expediency . . . cursed be the wealth which comes to use at such a price! Blessed be the poverty which gives us immunity from temptations.[47]

The ministers of the South urged their flocks to maintain their pride, solidarity, and resist the new temptations being suggested by the "brazen standard of money-making."

As W. J. Cash noted, most Southerners preferred their religious theology simple—with a clear metaphorical linkage in black-and-white images to explain cultural events. Richard Weaver broadened this notion to suggest that Southerners looked up to the highly respected rhetors in

---

[47]Woodward, *Origins of the New South*, 172.

the post-war era and expected them to provide a metaphoric vision to direct the future action of all.

Before the War, the economic certainty provided by the plantation system and Great Chain of Being social philosophy offered a comforting rhetoric, an ordered hierarchy of meaning for most Southerners. As the post-war economic era dawned, Southerners still held to the religious hierarchy and agrarian authority that has so dominated their past.[48] Any rhetor seeking the attention of the Southern mind in the 1880s would need to heed the strong appeal to metaphorical comparisons of the past. Fred Hobson has suggested that the consistent use of these religious and economic metaphors demonstrated a uniquely Southern obsession to explain defeat and failure to the rest of the nation.[49] This is one possibility, but the Southern rhetorical tradition was strong no matter what the particular circumstances of the suffering. The significance of the Southern brand of metaphor lies in the fact that the South endured a distinctive break in its historical fabric. The Southern audience needed a rhetoric charged with the energy to reorganize its thinking. As Edie has suggested, the only way rhetors could do this would be to use metaphors of historical comparison. Because of the unique evolution of the Southern church and economy, any regional speaker devoted to a mission of linking the South's romantic past to a positive, but different future would need to comprehend the distinctiveness and diversity of Southern metaphors as it entered the 1880s.[50] Henry W. Grady and Thomas E. Watson were two Southerners who were deeply steeped in this tradition and were prepared to speak about the challenges of the South's future.

---

[48]See, for example, Samuel S. Hill, *Religion and the Solid South* (Nashville, Abingdon Press, 1972) 184-85.

[49]Fred Hobson, *Tell About the South: The Southern Rage to Explain* (Baton Rouge: Louisiana State University Press, 1983) 12-13.

[50]Carl N. Degler, *Place Over Time: The Continuity of Southern Distinctiveness* (Baton Rouge: Louisiana State University Press, 1977) 126-27.

The Early Life of Henry W. Grady

Henry Woodfin Grady was born in Athens, Georgia, on April 24, 1850. The town of Athens, with a population of only 3,500, had been in existence for only forty-eight years before Grady's birth. The Georgia General Assembly specifically chose Athens as home for the University of Georgia in 1801 because of its "isolated and sinless" nature.[51] Grady was born in a white-columned mansion near the center of Athens, and the broad porch of the Grady home looked out from a small hill onto the university campus.

The young Grady was soon attending Methodist Sunday school and learning to read at a private school run by the daughter of the University of Georgia's President. Grady's education was interrupted in 1861 by the opening shots at Fort Sumter. Although his family generally favored the Union and voted for the moderate Democratic candidates, Grady's father volunteered to fight as a Captain in the Virginia campaigns.

On January 5, 1866, Grady was admitted to the sophomore class of the reopened University of Georgia based on his extensive personal reading during the war. One of the attributes that made Grady such an outstanding student was his extraordinary memory. After one reading, the young Georgian was able to repeat a page of print almost word for word.[52]

Soon after entering the university, Grady discovered that every student was required to join one of the two literary or debating societies on the campus. The Phi Kappa and Demosthenian societies held weekly meetings on Saturdays and provided college students of all class levels structured programs for declamation and debate.[53] Grady joined the Phi Kappa society and noted many years afterwards that this organization provided "the most valuable training" of his college career.[54] The young orator threw himself into the practice of debating to such an extent that

---

[51]Raymond B. Nixon, *Henry W. Grady: Spokesman of the New South* (New York: Alfred A. Knopf, 1943) 33.

[52]Marvin G. Bauer, "Henry W. Grady," in Vol. 1. of *A History and Criticism of American Public Address,* ed. Brigance, 397.

[53]E. Merton Coulter, *College Life in the Old South* (New York: Macmillan, 1928) 133-35.

[54]Nixon, *Henry W. Grady: Spokesman of the New South,* 42.

he was occasionally fined for "talking without permission" on the key point of a resolution. Even from these early weekly experiences, it is quite apparent that Grady soon became an accomplished practitioner of oratory. The faculty chose him as one of the eighteen sophomore orators at the 1866 commencement. Like his fellow Phi Kappas, Grady looked to the classical rhetorical models of Greece and Rome for instruction. The library of the literary society was a special source of pride for its members. The Phi Kappa library was so large, in fact, that it effectively rivaled the university's by containing an estimated 2,600 volumes.[55]

As the date of Grady's graduation from the University of Georgia neared, he received one of the highest honors then available to students. He was elected unanimously as Phi Kappa's commencement orator. For this grand occasion, Grady delivered a speech on "Castles in the Air" in which he "painted a vision for the future of the South."[56] The manuscript of this particular speech has not survived, but, as the graduation ceremonies came to an end, it was evident that Grady's speech had been a "hit" and that he was well on his way to becoming a local and national advocate for his native region.

Shortly after Grady's graduation, the triumphant orator was put under some pressure from the University of Georgia Chancellor to remain in Athens and start work on a master's degree. But Grady decided to attend the University of Virginia. One of the motivating factors drawing Grady to the campus at Charlottesville was his admiration of Thomas Jefferson. Grady believed that this historic institution had a reputation as a "principal training ground for southern leaders and their sons."[57]

Grady registered for graduate courses at Virginia in modern languages, history, literature, and rhetoric in the Fall of 1868. The major "consuming ambition of Grady from the day he arrived on the Virginia campus" was to be the final orator of the Washington Literary Society.[58] This "final" orator would be the Society's principal speaker during Spring Commencement, and Grady and his fellow club members coveted this position. Grady spent most of his free time outside his graduate classes practicing and preparing for his destiny as a final orator. On the final

---

[55]Coulter, 171.

[56]Nixon, 52. See also Harold E. Davis, *Henry Grady's New South: Atlanta A Brave and Beautiful City* (Tuscaloosa: University of Alabama Press, 1990) 30.

[57]As cited by Nixon, 54.

[58]Nixon, 56.

night of the March elections for the Washingtonians' orators, Grady learned that he lost the first spot by a mere three votes. This defeat was a great personal shock. Soon after losing the election, Grady decided not only to leave the Washingtonian Society, but the University of Virginia graduate program as well.[59] The defeated orator returned to Athens and spent a long summer of great introspection. Near the end of this personal exile, Grady made some important decisions about his future career. From his earliest years as an avid reader, he had been fond of the literary style of Charles Dickens. During that long summer of 1869, Grady discovered the writings of Brett Hart, whom he called an "American Dickens." Convinced now that a political career was out of his reach with the defeat at Virginia, Grady made the decision to become a journalist.[60]

As the summer slowly turned into fall, Grady began to submit newsy letters to several Southern newspapers such as the Atlanta *Constitution*. Isaac W. Avery, the Editor of the *Constitution*, enthusiastically accepted Grady's submissions for publication. Later in the fall during the busy harvest and festival season, Grady accepted invitations from Avery to cover local events for the fast-growing Atlanta newspaper. From contacts made on these assignments, Grady accepted his first regular newspaper position as associate editor of the Rome, Georgia *Courier*. At this small north Georgia newspaper, Grady apprenticed in journalism and thus laid the groundwork for a bright future in this profession.

The Early Life of Thomas E. Watson

The background of Thomas Edward Watson closely parallels that of the slightly older Grady. Watson was born on September 5, 1856 in a log house about three miles north of Thomson, Georgia in the east central part of the state. This area was then part of Columbia County. It was not until 1870 that this sparsely settled area would be formed into the much smaller McDuffie County with Thomson as its county seat.[61]

The frontier aura of Thomson during the 1860s was made even more difficult by the harshness of military Reconstruction. Before McDuffie

---

[59]Nixon, 62-63; and Davis, 31-32.

[60]See Bauer, 397; and Nixon, 62-63.

[61]William W. Brewton, *The Life of Thomas E. Watson*, (Atlanta: The Author, 1926) 11.

County was formally created in 1870, the area was well known for its political corruption.[62] On special occasions, Watson accompanied his father into Thomson and frequently was the witness of eye-gougings, knifings, and drunken brawls that were so often the rule in the area.

Before the Civil War, Watson's grandfather had owned 1,372 acres of land and forty-five slaves. These totals had made the elder Watson a relatively wealthy man for that area of Georgia. After Appomattox, when other Georgia planters were struggling to feed their families, Thomas's father built a massive new plantation home on the old family land and tried to support his large family with money from cotton harvested by white labor. But John Smith Watson, who had been wounded twice during the war, quickly amassed large debts, and, in 1868, the grand house was sold to pay creditors. He then moved the family to a modest farm outside of Thomson.

In spite of the great decline in his family's fortunes, Tom Watson managed to receive an education in a local field school near Thomson. Watson's mother, Ann, devoted much of her time to teaching her son history and biography. Mrs. Watson was especially interested in French history and passed on much of this interest to her son.[63] With his mother's encouragement, Watson soon became an avid reader. By the time he was fifteen, the youth had written down an impressive list of books that he had read. The list covered five pages in his large diary and included such classic works as: Homer, Shakespeare, Byron, Milton, Wordsworth, Poe, Pope, and Goldsmith. Besides these works, Watson also included the popular novels of Scott, Dickens, Defoe, and Irving. In the area of history, Watson recorded as having read Goodrich's histories of Rome, England, and the United States; Goldsmith's histories of Greece and England; and Alexander Stephens's *War Between the States*.[64] This extensive reading list also demonstrated Watson's early interest in the art of rhetoric. His diary indicated that he had read Cox's *Reading and Speaking*, Magoon's *Living Orators and Orators of America*, and Francis's *Orators of the Age*.

When Watson's school term of 1872 ended, he made it known to his family that he wished to travel to Macon in the fall and attend Mercer

---

[62]C. Vann Woodward, *Tom Watson: Agrarian Rebel* (London: Oxford University Press, 1938) 15.

[63]Brewton, 16.

[64]Woodward, *Tom Watson*, 24; and Brewton, 41-44.

University. This desire to enter college, even though he had not yet finished the local school at his tender age of 15 seemed prompted by the decision to follow his favorite teacher, E. A. Steed, to this same institution.[65]

Tom Watson enrolled at Mercer as a freshman in October, 1872. Mercer University was a small Baptist college that had been founded with the solemn purpose of promoting "the education of poor young men preparing for the ministry." When Tom Watson enrolled at the college, there were only five professors. Professor Steed held the Chair of Latin and became Watson's best friend while he was in Macon. Under the professor's influence, Watson joined the Mercer chapter of the Phi Delta debating society. At the regular weekly meetings of this society, Watson could flaunt his learning and bring to use his extensive collection of quotations which he was always copying into his scrapbooks and personal diary.[66] During his sophomore year, he began recording his college experiences in a large diary. In this large ledger-sized volume, Watson began paying special devotion to his "Ideal Goddess"—Eloquence.

Watson regarded the study of oratory as the major art to be acquired in his schooling, and it was his most cherished ambition to master it. In his diary, he carefully copied down whole texts for speeches or extensive notes for future orations. For example, he devoted an entire page of his journal to "Hints on Oratory Taught by Experience—Not Books." In the twelve points he wrote down on the art, Watson demonstrated his close familiarity with the classical rhetorical canons. Point twelve was "To pay ardent, unceasing adoration to her as an ideal goddess, at whose touch the human heart thrives with joy, throbs with enthusiasm, melts with pity, trembles with fear, droops with woe, burns with indignation, or stands in mute horror."[67]

In Watson's recorded speeches delivered before the Phi Delta Society, he revealed how closely he had studied the art of oratory. While Demosthenes was a favorite, Watson speculated upon his own theory for how to use pathos when addressing the typical American audience. For a "public democratical speech," Watson's recipe was to end the speech

---

[65]Woodward, *Tom Watson*, 24-25.

[66]Ibid., 28-29.

[67]Thomas E. Watson Papers, Southern Historical Collection, University of North Carolina at Chapel Hill, *Journal #2*, 130.

"with a grand Spread Eagle." The specific rhetorical philosophy advocated by Watson in this youthful diary was to recognize that

> when the national heart is heaving with excitement, he who would control its pulsations and direct its energies, must speak the language of enthusiasm. The power of the orator lies in the sympathy between him and the people. This is the chord which finds heart to heart; and when struck, thousands burst into tears or rouse into passion, like a single individual.[68]

From the extensive notes made by Watson during his two years at Mercer, it was evident that he enjoyed the practice of eloquence most of all. By mastering the art of oratory, Watson hoped to become a prominent man. But, by the end of his sophomore year, the original loan taken out by Watson's mother expired, and he returned home due to a lack of money.

Throughout the summer following his return to Thomson, Watson was unable to find work. The family soon abandoned the farm and tried a new start in the relatively large city of Augusta, Georgia. In September, with his financial situation and that of his family desperate, Watson had to sell his book collection at a public auction. This forced liquidation of his beloved books—along with the hasty move off his family's land and into an unfriendly city—created intense personal despair for the young Watson who was barely eighteen years old. After Tom discussed leaving the family to find work in Texas, his mother Ann came to his rescue; she obtained permission for Tom to read law in the office of Judge W. R. McLaws of Augusta. After two years of training in law, Watson left Augusta for rural Screven County and, within a year, returned to his hometown of Thomson determined to find his fame as an attorney.

---

[68]As cited in Woodward, *Tom Watson*, 28.

Chapter 2

Henry Grady's Vision

"Under the leadership of Grady . . . the South moved back into the radiance of that central temple of a unified people's faith; and also began to carry a torch of freedom from the old and discarded modes."

—Francis P. Gaines
Southern Oratory: A Study in Idealism

Born and educated to be a part of the Southern elite, Henry W. Grady was well aware of the rhetorical tradition and its importance to a Southern audience. Besides his formal training as an orator, Grady's journalism career forced him to develop skills as an acute observer of Southern history.

This chapter will trace the early journalism experiences of Grady and will critique his major ceremonial speeches with a special attention to metaphors as they appear at important junctures in his speeches. The specific focus here will be a close synthesis of the metaphors or vivid figures of speech linked by Grady to suggestions for improving the Southern economy and for changes in lifestyle required of Southerners. The chapter will conclude with an assessment of what Grady's use of metaphors during this historical era may suggest about the visionary thinking he had concerning the South's future.

Grady Matures as Editor and Speaker

On Monday morning, September 6, 1869, Henry W. Grady reported to the offices of the Rome, Georgia *Courier* as the newspaper's new associate editor. The young journalist immediately began a series of editorial attacks against the administration of Georgia Governor Rufus B. Bullock. After the Civil War, the state government had been in the hands of Radical Reconstructionists, and Bullock, elected in 1868, attempted more moderate path toward restoring the Georgia economy. Bullock called for state-supported internal improvements financed primarily by draining

capital from agriculture.[1] Grady's first editorials for the *Courier* denounced Bullock's lavish spending for special party trains and governmental
balls.[2] Grady and the *Courier* staff devoted themselves to the coverage
of Georgia politics; Bullock, and most Georgia Republicans, came under
regular editorial attack from Grady's pen.

After serving ten months as associate editor, Grady became upset
with the conservative politics of his publisher and decided to buy his own
newspaper. Even though Rome was a small town in the hills of north
Georgia with a population of less than three thousand, it did have three
newspapers. Grady purchased the Rome *Commercial* and assumed control
as editor and publisher on July 29, 1870. Soon after Grady took over, the
Commercial's circulation began to climb due to close supportive coverage
of north Georgia's Ku Klux Klan activities. By May 1871, Grady felt
financially secure enough to buy out the third Rome newspaper, the
Daily. As now the sole rival to the *Courier*, Grady's *Commercial* soon
became the largest newspaper in north Georgia.[3]

Grady came to dominate journalism in his region of the state and
soon sought out a larger challenge for his editorial talents. On October
21, 1872, Grady became co-owner of the Atlanta *Herald*. After selling all
interests in the *Commercial* to his former boss at the *Courier*, Grady
moved to the rebuilding city of Atlanta.

When Grady arrived in the editorial offices of the *Herald*, it was with
the recognition that his financial battles to keep the newspaper alive
would not bring easy victories. As the thriving railroad hub of the entire
South, Atlanta had a population of 30,000 in 1872.[4] The growing city,
forced to almost completely rebuild itself from Sherman's torch, boasted
of two other morning newspaper besides the *Herald*, the *Constitution* and
the *Sun*. Grady moved quickly to establish the name of his small paper,
running lead articles on page one on "Crime." The co-owner of the
Herald, Alexander St. Clair-Abrams, a former editor of the New York
Herald, convinced Grady to establish a pattern of sensationalism

---

[1]Numan Bartley, *The Creation of Modern Georgia* (Athens: University of Georgia
Press, 1983) 60-61.

[2]Raymond B. Nixon, *Henry W. Grady: Spokesman of the New South* (New York:
Alfred A. Knopf, 1943) 71-73.

[3]Nixon, 85. See also Harold E. Davis, *Henry Grady's New South: Atlanta, A
Brave and Beautiful City* (Tuscaloosa: University of Alabama Press, 1990) 32-33.

[4]Nixon, 95.

throughout the early issues of the newspaper. With crime and disaster stories as its basic staple, the Atlanta *Herald* attempted to maintain a middle political course between the pro-liberal Republican *Constitution*, and the traditional Southern Democratic *Sun*.

On June 24, 1873, the *Sun* suspended publication. Grady and his financial partners moved quickly to intensify the *Herald's* circulation war with the *Constitution*. Both newspapers became engaged in expensive efforts to expand their circulations beyond the Atlanta area by chartering special trains southward to Macon, Georgia. Within a few months, this crippling competition forced Grady to cut back his expansion efforts. When his financial partner Abrams retired from the newspaper, Grady acquired a new partner, Robert A. Alston. Even with the additional financial help of Alston, Grady's newspaper slowly lost ground in its battle with the *Constitution*. By February 6, 1876, a legal advertisement in the *Constitution* announced a sheriff's sale of the *Herald* publishing company.[5]

After only limited success with newspapers in Atlanta, Grady had to accept the writing jobs offered to him. As he had done as a college student, Grady took part-time jobs with various state newspapers reporting on Atlanta events. In a desperate attempt to secure regular employment, Grady made the long train trip from Atlanta to New York to seek a position at the prestigious New York *Herald*. After a personal interview with the *Herald* editor, Thomas B. Connery, Grady became the sole Atlanta correspondent for the New York paper.

As prestigious as his new position may have been, Grady made very little money writing "string stories" for the New York *Herald*. The Atlanta reporter was paid space rates, which meant that he received payment only for those stories the New York paper had column space for. Since Atlanta news was seldom of sufficient national interest to command much space in the *Herald*, Grady remained financially strapped. Fortunately, during the fall of 1876, Evan P. Howell purchased half interest in the Atlanta *Constitution* and sought out Grady to be part of his editorial staff. On October 19, 1876, Grady formally began his duties as an editorial writer for the *Constitution*.[6]

As a well-known editor of the *Constitution*, Grady was invited to give lectures and speeches to various groups around the city. From 1877

---

[5]Nixon, 118.
[6]Nixon, 126-27; See also Davis, 36-37.

to 1878, Grady served as an active member of the Lecture Committee of the Young Men's Library Association.[7] Grady made a considerable income as an entertaining or "human interest" lecturer, but he had given this up by the end of the summer of 1878 to do more free-lance writing for national magazines such as *Harper's*.

In his columns in the *Constitution*, Grady moved away from political and human interest topics to issues that were closer to his heart. On February 13, 1881, for example, Grady lashed out at Northern fiction writers for creating in the popular mind two false stereotypes of Southerners:

> the long-haired, livid faced, slave-driver with uplifted whip and attendant bloodhounds, and the profligate planter whose passion rides in his blood and who spends money as easily as he spills blood.[8]

In 1880, Grady purchased a quarter interest in the *Constitution* and became the newspaper's managing editor. Under his leadership, the Atlanta paper grew rapidly. Even though his management duties often distracted him from writing columns, Grady did continue to express his views infrequently on page one in a space entitled "Man About Town." During elections or other events calling for interpretative news stories, Grady contributed essays signed "H.W.G."[9]

From 1881 to 1886, Grady and his editorial staff of the *Constitution* worked diligently in local city charity projects as well as state politics. With his own writing time at a premium, Grady allowed two members of his editorial staff, N. P. I. Finch and Joel Chandler Harris, to write most editorials on national and international affairs.[10] One assignment that Grady would not pass off to another writer: coverage of Atlanta's professional baseball club. In the spring of 1885, Grady inspired the creation of Atlanta's team and became the first president of the Southern Baseball League.[11]

---

[7]Marvin G. Bauer, "Henry Grady," in Vol. 1 of *A History and Criticism of American Public Address*, ed. Brigance, 398.

[8]The *Atlanta Constitution*, 13 February 1881, 1.

[9]Nixon, 207; See also Davis, 52-53.

[10]Nixon, 213.

[11]Nixon, 224-25.

In the election year of 1886, Grady became involved in Georgia politics by urging former Confederate General John B. Gordon to run for Governor. Serving as the old general's campaign advisor, Grady arranged for Gordon to deliver a speech on the same platform in Atlanta as Jefferson Davis, the occasion being the formal unveiling of a statue of former Georgia Governor, Benjamin H. Hill.

On April 25, 1886, with Grady as master of ceremonies, almost the entire population of Atlanta turned out for the dedication of the Hill monument. According to the *Constitution*, over 90,000 people gathered at the intersection of Peachtree, West Peachtree, and Baker Streets to hear Davis and Gordon deliver speeches in honor of Hill.[12]

The carefully staged ceremony helped to elect Gordon Governor. Grady's planning, however, had different effects outside the South. A crowd in Albany, New York, for example, sang "We'll hang Jeff Davis to a Sour Apple Tree." A large group of irate citizens in Ohio actually hung the former Confederate President in effigy. The New York *Tribune*, shortly after the events in Atlanta, editorially attacked Davis as an "unrepentant old villain and union hater."[13]

The Congressional elections of 1886, like the Governor's race in Georgia, rekindled a national concern with Southern pride. While Gordon was emphasizing in his speeches a close devotion to the principles of the "old South" by urging Georgians to "hold to the characteristics of our old civilization,"[14] Grady became concerned that this message would have the wrong effect in the North.

With the end of Reconstruction in 1877, Southern Democrats like Gordon usually ran without opposition. The national Republican Party, however, was determined to return to power and carrying the South was seen as a necessity. In order to win the South, the Republicans knew that capturing the black vote would be essential. This was difficult, however, in light of the passage of Jim Crow laws throughout the South that effectively disenfranchised the Negro.[15] When blacks did attempt to vote in Southern elections, violence would often erupt. Reports of these violent lynchings and near riots were frequently even more exaggerated in the

---

[12]The *Atlanta Constitution*, 26 April 1886, 1; See also Davis, 82-83.

[13]As cited in Nixon, 230.

[14]Bartley, *The Creation of Modern Georgia,* 107.

[15]C. Vann Woodward, *Origins of the New South* (Baton Rouge: Louisiana State University Press, 1953) 55-56.

Republican-controlled press in most Northern states. Newspaper reports of violence throughout the South tended to make Northern investors wary of aiding development in the region.[16]

One Northern industrialist concerned with sectional strife was John H. Inman of New York. As director of the Richmond and Danville Railroad Company, Inman's trains travelled the important line between Washington, D.C. and Atlanta. It was Inman who suggested to George F. Baker and H. C. Fahvestock, two influential New York bankers and members of the New England Society, that they invite Grady to address their Society as a "progressive young Southerner" with a "reassuring message to the North."[17] On November 6, 1886, the Atlanta editor received the invitation to address the New England Society of New York City. Grady accepted the invitation and travelled to New York to deliver his reassuring message on December 21, 1886. Grady outlined his concept of where the South had come from and where the South should go; this was the first speech in which he provided a glimpse of his futuristic vision.

The New South Speech

The meeting of the New England Society of New York City on December 21, 1886, was held in the banquet hall of Delmonico's Cafe with 360 guests invited to attend. The dinner celebrated the 266th anniversary of the landing of the Pilgrims at Plymouth Rock and the speaker's table at the front of the room was filled with very important guests. Seated in places of honor were Grady, General William T. Sherman, J. Pierpoint Morgan, and Lyman Abbot. After a prayerful speech from Dr. T. DeWitt Talmage, General Sherman rose to offer a few short remarks about his Civil War experiences. As soon as the general finished, the orchestra in the balcony burst into a rendition of "Marching Through Georgia." Once the room had returned to order, the President of the Society introduced Grady.

The Georgian began his speech by quoting from Benjamin Hill: "There was a South of slavery and secession—that South is dead. There

---

[16]Woodward, 56-57; and Nixon, 237-38.

[17]Nixon, 238; See also Davis, 175-76.

is a South of union and freedom—that South, thank God, is living, breathing, growing every hour."[18] From this opening statement, Grady's metaphors suggest a new genesis for the people of the South. The old stereotyped images that Northerners might associate with the South were now lifeless, according to the Grady metaphors, and a freshly born Southern child was ready to take on the challenges of life.

After trying to demonstrate sectional and vital unity with his opening quotation, Grady moved on to tell two jokes to relax his New York audience and to "beg" his listeners to "bring full faith in American fairness and frankness to judgment upon what I am about to say." Grady then stressed his sectional unity imagery by recalling the "Cavalier" label for Southerners and the "Puritan" title for Northerners. He reminded his audience that it was a Cavalier, John Smith, who "gave New England its very name."[19] These labels identifying regional personalities were "lost in the storm of the first Revolution, and the American citizen" title supplanted both. Grady transformed the separate images of the Northerner and Southerner into the grand "citizen" metaphor in order to minimize their regional differences and to emphasize their patriotic similarities.

In Grady's emerging vision, the "union" of the separate colonists— Puritans and Cavaliers—slowly perfected themselves like "valuable plants." The example of the best flowering of this unity was the true American, Abraham Lincoln. After paying homage to the martyred president, Grady moved to visualize for his audience what the typical Southerner returned home to find after Appomattox. Grady noted the Southern soldier struggled home to find

> his home in ruins, his farm devastated, his slaves free, his stock killed, his barns empty, his trade destroyed, his money worthless, his social system, feudal in its magnificence, swept away; his people without law or legal status; his comrades slain, and the burdens of others heavy on his shoulders. Crushed by defeat, very traditions are gone.[20]

---

[18]Joel Chandler Harris, *Life of Henry W. Grady Including His Writings and Speeches* (New York: Cassel Publishing, 1890) 83. This text is identical to that in the *New York Tribune*, 22 December 1886, 1.

[19]Harris, 85.

[20]Harris, 86-87. Also quoted by Davis, 177.

Even as Grady painted metaphorically this picture of Southern defeat, he quickly suggested to his audience that these facts were not cause for despair. Instead of sullenness, Grady stated that the Southerner, who had been stripped by God of prosperity, would now be inspired by the heavenly Father in these times of adversity and change. As evidence of the transition, Grady pointed out that:

> The soldier stepped from the trenches into the furrow; horses that had charged Federal guns marched before the plow, and fields that ran red with human blood in April were green with the harvest in June. Women reared in luxury cut up their dresses and made breeches for their husbands, and, with a patience and heroism that fit women always as a garment, gave their hands to work.[21]

The antebellum landscape that might have been common to the thinking of most Northerners about the South was transformed by Grady's metaphors into one dominated by a new breed of hard-working ex-soldiers. These former Cavaliers felt "no bitterness" toward the North and worked to rebuild a different life than they had known before the war. From a battlefield of death, Grady once again stressed that a new kind of Southern life was taking root in a resurrected and reborn land.

In order to explain the "sum of work" that Southerners had been engaged in since the war, Grady argued that "we have planted the schoolhouse on the hilltop and made it free to black and white. We have sowed towns and cities in place of theories, and put business above politics."[22] The harvest of results from the newly transformed South was even now prepared to "challenge spinners in Massachusetts and iron-makers from Pennsylvania." With these growing achievements, Grady contended that the reconstructed and reborn Southerner "had fallen in love with work."

Once he had described work in vivid rhetorical figures, Grady moved directly into a discussion of the change since slavery was prevalent in the South. While the "Old South" had rested everything on slavery and agriculture, Grady emphasized that the New South presented a "perfect democracy" with "a hundred farms for every plantation, fifty homes for every palace—and a diversified industry" that would meet the "complex need of a new complex age." The New South would no longer be held

---

[21]Harris, 87.
[22]Harris, 88.

back by slavery and large farms but would allow her soul to be stirred with the "breath of a new life." In Grady's conclusion, the renewed and reorganized life-form that had been the South was not a mere wilting plant; it was an upright, fully blossoming new life unleashed to take on an unlimited future.[23] This new creation emerging from the ashes of the Old South was prepared to think "all one way" with her brothers of the North.

It was almost midnight when Grady had finished his speech. The next morning, however, most major New York newspapers devoted much space to praising the "New South" speech with the grandest hyperbole.[24] Reporters specifically applauded the speech as important in helping to unify North and South with a common appeal to industrial growth. Grady's vision for the South's future, however, was not yet complete. The success of the "New South" speech resulted in Grady being offered many opportunities to further explain his perspective on North-South relations. Through most of 1887 and the greater part of 1888, Grady had to decline many invitations outside of Atlanta to speak because of the demand of his job at the *Constitution*.[25]

The election year of 1888 found Grady involved in the early campaigns of many of Georgia's Democratic candidates. As a candidate himself for the post of Democratic presidential elector, Grady decided not to limit himself to speeches in Georgia. On October 27, Grady accepted an invitation to speak at the Texas State Fair in Dallas on the topic, "The South and Its Problems."

Grady's Dallas Speech

Before leaving Atlanta to deliver his speech in Dallas, Henry Grady took steps to enhance the national newspaper coverage that the speech might receive. The editor wrote out the speech he intended to deliver so that proof-sheets might be mailed in advance to newspapers around the country.[26] On October 23, Grady left for Dallas aboard a private train.

---

[23]Harris, 91.

[24]For reactions to the speech, see Nixon, 247-53 and Davis, 178-79.

[25]See Nixon, 255-58.

[26]Harris, 285-86. See also the personal diary of Telamon Cuyler's recording the events of this Dallas trip in the Henry W. Grady Papers, Special Collections Department, Emory University (Atlanta GA), Box 1, Folder #10.

There was a strong sense of thematic continuity between Grady's New York and Dallas speeches because of two situational factors. First, the rostrum from which Grady spoke at the Fair was extended, an arch being a quotation from the earlier New South speech: "We have sowed cities in place of theories." A second connection to the New England Society speech was the beginning of the Dallas speech in which Grady again quoted Benjamin H. Hill: "Who saves his country, saves all things, and all things saved will bless him. Who lets his country die, lets all things die, and all things dying curse him."[27]

After paying respect to the "first city of the grandest state of the greatest government on this earth," Grady explained that certain issues which "strike deeper" than any political theory needed to be addressed. He proposed to explore the problems of the South without regards to "party limitations" or political motives. Taking a key rhetorical question, Grady pondered aloud "What held the Southern states together?" He argued that if this unity was based on a vague sense of "sectionalism," then this hatred of the North must be "rooted out of our hearts." Since the devastation of the South during the war had been so complete, Grady observed that Southerners must realize that:

> In all the past, there is nothing to draw them into an essential or lasting alliance—nothing in all that heroic record that can not be rendered unfearing from provincial hands into the keeping of American history.[28]

The important problem to be overcome in the South's future was the existence of "two separate races" nearly equal in numbers residing in the region. The South had nothing to fear from former slaves, Grady pointed out. As proof of the "negro's faith and loyalty," Grady explained that during the war, with five hundred Negroes to a single white woman, no acts of violence were recorded against women or children. The loyal companionship shown by the former slaves to their former masters provided the "root" that "sprang some foliage" of support during the war.

---

[27]Harris, 94. This text also appeared in the *Dallas Morning News*, 28 October 1888, 17-18; and in the *Atlanta Constitution*, 28 October 1888, 10-12. It should be noted that Harris incorrectly cites the date of the speech as "1887." See also Ferald J. Bryan, "Henry Grady and Southern Ideology: An Analysis of the Texas State Fair Address," in *Rhetoric and Ideology: Compositions and Criticisms of Power*, ed. Kneupper, 205-11.

[28]Harris, 96.

But, even with the historical basis of cooperation, Grady moved to the core of the Southerner's concern with the race issue—voting.

With an unmistakable metaphorical reference to the inferiority of Negroes, Grady declared that he was not in favor of "dividing the vote" along white and black lines. He stated:

> The worst thing, in my opinion, that could happen is the white people of the South should stand in opposing factions, with the vast mass of ignorant or purchasable votes between.[29]

Grady believed that, above all, the white race must continue to hold domination over the Negro throughout the South. His metaphors presented a picture of a post-Reconstruction Great Chain of Being for Southern society. The white Southerner must stay politically unified since control now hinged on the "integrity of its own vote and the largest of its sympathy and justice which it shall compel the support of the better classes of the colored races." With metaphorical frankness, he assured his audience that

> the supremacy of the white race of the South must be maintained forever, and the domination of the negro race resisted at all points and at all hazards—because the white race is the superior race. This is the declaration of no new truth. It has abided forever in the marrow of our bones, and shall run forever with the blood that feed Anglo-Saxon hearts.[30]

The racial relationship was an act of God, and no mortal man had the right to "tinker with the work of the Almighty." This fact in Grady's mind was unchangeable and therefore was not a sectional issue. The new creation that he had previously described as emerging from the ruins of war not only had a reordered perspective on how to view the working world, but the blood of this new creature's veins surged with that of the historically dominant Anglo-Saxon. Grady noted that this type of blood had, through the ages, been in the veins of "Alfred the Great, Oliver Cromwell, Napoleon," and ultimately "established this republic, carved it from the wilderness, conquered it from the Indians, wrestled it from

---

[29]Harris, 99.
[30]Harris, 100.

England, and at last, stilling its own tumult, consecrated it forever as the home of the Anglo-Saxon."[31]

Grady laid the source of the South's problem regarding race at the feet of the Republican Party. In Grady's vision, the Republicans of the North sought to "dominate these southern states through the colored vote." To counter this plot, Grady argued that "some brave statesman" must feel moved to question "the stranger at our gates" and exclude all of those "seeking to plant anarchy or to establish alien men or measures" on Southern soil.

In the first half of Grady's Dallas speech, his metaphors cast Negroes in a most inferior and threatening light. The deficiency of the black race was historically demonstrated and metaphorically linked to the Great Chain of Being ideology that was very familiar to Grady's Southern audience. Finally, the editor observed that dealing with the race problem might prove to be a blessing for the South because "the race that threatened our ruin [would] work our salvation as it fills our fields with the best peasantry the world has ever seen."[32] These implications, coming just before Grady began discussing the industrial problems of the South, suggested that Negroes should remain "in their place" so that white Southerners could leave the land and seek other new horizons. Since the blood of the Negro was not of the quality needed to rise above tilling the land, Grady concluded this section of his speech by stating that former slaves should remain on the farms while white Southerners pursued a solution to the South's industrial problem.

The first major point Grady stressed about the South's industrial capability was that in the twenty years since the war, Southerners had "given willingly six hundred million dollars as pensions for northern soldiers." As significant as this total was, Grady explained that the Southern "soldier-farmer," in the years since Appomattox, had harvested a crop worth over eight hundred million dollars. From this bounty, the South had rebuilt her cities and recouped her losses. After establishing the capabilities of the Southern "soldier-farmer," Grady provided an important metaphorical bridge of symbolic associative meaning for the economic future of his Southern audience. He said:

---

[31]Harris, 102.
[32]Harris, 105.

For ten years the world has been at peace. The pioneer has now replaced the soldier. Commerce has whitened new seas, and the merchant has occupied new areas. Steam has made of the earth a chessboard, on which the men must play for markets.[33]

In the aftermath of Reconstruction, Grady was now emphasizing for his Dallas listeners that the industrial world had changed and the Southern cotton farmer must change with it. Cotton was still the dominant crop throughout the South and the yearly harvest was exceptional. With the growing success of cotton production, Grady pointed out that the South's monopoly on the world market was not seriously threatened from foreign markets. Grady asserted that the Southern share of the cotton market would continue to grow because as the American missionary "woos the heathen with a cotton shirt in one hand and a Bible in the other," the demand for the South's crop would only grow. However, while the overall production of cotton was up, the prices that farmers were paid were still very low. Grady's combination of economic and religious imagery at this juncture was an effort to project a more hopeful future demand for cotton.

Besides a wealth of cotton, Grady also indicated that the South had iron and coal in abundant supply. From these two basic staples of industry, Grady launched a metaphorical flourish:

Think of it! In cotton a monopoly. In coal and iron establishing a swift mastery. In granite and marble developing equal advantage and resource. In yellow pine and hard woods the world's treasury. Surely the basis of the South's wealth and power is laid by the hand of the Almighty God, and its prosperity has been established by divine law.[34]

With such great resources, it was Grady's conclusion that divine will ordained that the South enter the worldwide chess match for markets. In order to insure success in this game for Southerners, he had two specific recommendations for his Dallas audience. First, he argued that the South must abandon one-crop farming. As prosperous as cotton had made some Southern farmers, the editor contended that this single crop could not support a city or community because there was no "artisan or mechanic"

---

[33]Harris, 106.
[34]Harris, 109.

work to attract immigrants. These immigrants were needed not only as a market for staple crops, but to build "trucks for the farm."

In the Grady vision, the South must diversify its crops and attract new industry. As a model for his ideal state, Grady pointed to the Midwest where he believed "agriculture and manufactures" were set in a proper balance. As the South rapidly diversified its crops and diversified its industries, Grady concluded that this new economic strength would only "make broader the glory and deepen the majesty of the Union which reigns supreme in our hearts." This mission, however, could be fulfilled only if the people of the South heeded the call of the "Great Physician" who could lift them "up from trouble into content, from suffering into peace, from death into life."[35]

Grady ended the Dallas speech with the assertion that any future change would likely have Heavenly approval. The metaphorical contrast attached to the long-departed past and the unlimited potential of the future was set clearly in Grady's mind. The former soldier-farmer now had to transform himself into a merchant of the world market. This transition from agrarian planter to world tradesman was not only unavoidable because of the changes brought about by the war, but it was also the way God could perfect his Southern kingdom.

The Farmer's Place:
Grady's Speeches for Agrarian Reform

Once Grady returned to Atlanta from Texas, he was very distressed that his Dallas speech had received so little attention in the Northern press.[36] He was further depressed when he learned that Benjamin Harrison had defeated Grover Cleveland for the presidency. On top of these developments, Grady's wife suffered a miscarriage and he personally lost over five thousand dollars in a cotton speculation deal.[37] As Grady had in his

---

[35]Harris, 119.

[36]See Nixon, 290-91. The major daily newspapers of the day, the *New York Times*, the *New York Tribune*, and the *Chicago Tribune* failed to even mention the speech in their October 28, 1888 issues.

[37]See Nixon, 293-303. This depression is also confirmed from Grady's personal correspondence available in the Henry W. Grady Papers, Special Collections Department, Emory University (Atlanta GA), Box 1, Folders 1-4.

past personal defeats, he turned with intensity to his duties as editor of the *Constitution*.

In late 1889, Grady returned to the stump to address the deepening economic problems of Georgia's farmers. Cotton prices had dropped to an all-time low of eight and one-half cents and there was little relief in sight. Grady had long been concerned with the farmer's plight and turned down every invitation to speak in the North and West during the summer of 1889 in order to address the agrarian problem in Georgia. As far back as 1881, Grady had written an essay for *Harper's* magazine in which he had pondered the future of "Cotton and Its Kingdom."[38] In this article, Grady feared that the small Georgia farmer would be forced to the brink of serfdom by the credit and crop-lien system. Beginning in December 1888 and continuing through March 1889, Grady personally supervised a special page in the *Constitution* devoted to a discussion of the farm problem and the organizational efforts of agrarian reformers.[39]

As a perceptive journalist, Grady was well aware of the growing agitation of farmers' groups throughout the South. In one short speech delivered before the Southern Farmers' Alliance in August 1887, Grady declared that "if it be true that we are losing ground we will search for the mistakes and errors in our system and cast them out forever."[40] Grady addressed the problems of the farmer in a commencement speech to the Literary Societies of the University of Virginia on June 25, 1889.[41] Entitled "Against Centralization," Grady focused on what he believed to be the key barriers to success for Southern farmers. The two main forces allied against the farmers were oppressively high railroad shipping rates and tight credit restrictions from major Northern banks.

After apologizing for his "scanty time for preparation," Grady paid special tribute to the Civil War battlefields of Virginia whose "martyrdom made it the mecca" of loyal Southerners. But from these ancient glories, Grady reminded his audience of the coming "miracles of the Present." What could prevent the realization of the future Grady identified as a government that had become the "prey of spoilsmen" and trade that was

---

[38]Henry W. Grady, "Cotton and Its Kingdom," *Harper's New Monthly Magazine* 63 (October 1881): 719-34.

[39]Nixon, 308; the *Atlanta Constitution*, 26 June 1889, 1; and Davis, 111-17.

[40]The *Atlanta Constitution*, 17 August 1886, 1.

[41]In addition to the text in Harris, 142-57, the speech was originally printed in the *Atlanta Constitution*, 26 June 1889, 1.

in the "grasp of monopoly and commerce shackled with limitation."[42] In spite of these problems, Grady explained that these commercial restrictions should be overlooked so that the "great American heart" could continue to beat "undismayed."

In order to "rally the people to the defense of their liberties," Grady pleaded with his audience to act. Since the university served as the "training ground for the future," Grady argued that the students hearing the speech must realize that they could be "prophets of learning" for Southern farmers. As he outlined the particular mission for college students, Grady's metaphors were engaging:

> The farmer has learned that brains mix better with his soil than the waste of seabirds, and the professor walks by his side as he spreads the showers in the verdure of his field and locks the sunshine in the glory of the harvest. A button is pressed by a child's finger and the work of a million men is done. The hand is nothing—the brain everything. Physical prowess has had its day and the age of reason has come.[43]

While science was the way to overcome the difficulties of agrarian labor, Grady argued that implementation of these new revolutionary methods was threatened by the "increasing tendency to concentrate in the Federal Government powers and privileges that should be left to the states." Grady believed the root cause of the effort to centralize power in the government was "paternalism run mad." Through the Federal "control of the arteries of trade," select spoilsmen such as merchants and manufacturers were benefiting at the hands of the farmers.

By developing a strong, new patriotism, small farmers could effectively cope with the problem of centralized wealth. Grady stated that the citizen was a unit of the state and that a strong love of home should generate a self-protecting pride. Specifically, Grady recommended that every Southerner be taught that "his home is his castle, and that sovereignty rests beneath his hat." This new sense of personal pride would allow Southerners in the Grady vision to be "self-respecting, self-reliant, and responsible." He concluded his University of Virginia speech by pleading that individual citizens must cultivate small industries within

---

[42]Harris, 144.
[43]Harris, 145.

their own communities and let these localities be independent, or "sovereign to their own wants."

One month after addressing the literary societies at Virginia, Grady spoke to a group of farmers gathered on July 23, 1889 for a barbecue in Elberton, Georgia. In this speech, the editor continued to ponder out loud in metaphorical terms the proper role of the "Farmer and the City."[44]

As he began his speech, Grady made reference to most of his other public discourses by pointing out that this was the first time in his life that he spoke to an audience in the open air. Since all of Grady's earlier speeches had been delivered in grand halls, he stressed his appreciation for being able to speak outside in "God's majestic temple." With the meal being prepared in the foreground of the podium from which Grady spoke, he made reference to the fact that the dinner "covers more provisions than those issued to the soldiers of Lee's army."

Even though he promised to be brief, Grady warned his listeners that he felt compelled to speak on matters important to state and country. Every Saturday morning, Elberton included, Grady observed that farmers were organizing in "secret and serious session" to decide what to do about the "discriminating and oppressive forces" that threatened them. Grady summed up the reason these Southern farmers were joining such organizations as the Farmer's Alliance:

> It was not the skillful arts of the demagogue that has brought nearly two million farmers into this perfect and pledge-bound society—but it is a deep and abiding conviction that, in political and commercial economy of the day, he is put at a disadvantage that keeps him poor while others grow rich, and that bars his way to prosperity and independence.[45]

Grady believed that the reason farmers were organizing had substantial merit, but he argued that farmers and merchants must do their "patriotic duty" and stay politically unified. According to the Grady metaphor, the two groups were "brothers of a common mother, branded in common allegiance and marching to a common destiny." No matter what the problem was, Grady argued that there was "no room for divided hearts in this state, or in this Republic." From these not-so-subtle appeals

---

[44]This was the title of the speech as reprinted in Harris, 158-79; and the *Atlanta Constitution*, 26 July 1889, 1.

[45]Harris, 161-62.

for farmers to stay within the Democratic Party, Grady then turned to a detailed review of the problems that confronted Southern farmers.

After statistically demonstrating the rapid movement in population from country to city, Grady said that small towns and villages were vanishing while people migrated to the large cities of the South. Grady saw this development as a "great calamity." He stated:

> It saddens me to see a bright young fellow come to my office from village or country, and I shudder when I think for what a feverish and uncertain life he has bartered his rural birthright, and surrender the deliberation and tranquility of his life on the farm.[46]

Grady emphasized the new threats that would face the rural youth when he entered the new world of the city:

> In the corresponding growth of our cities—already center spots of danger, with their idle classes, their sharp rich and poor, their corrupt politics, their consorted thieves, and their clubs and societies of anarchy and socialism—I see a pressing danger.[47]

Grady cited the major reason for the migration away from the farms as the excessive weight of mortgages. In his estimate, more than one-fourth of the farms in Georgia were "in bondage to the money-lender." Grady reserved special metaphors for describing to his rural listeners the fear of losing a mortgage:

> A mortgage is the bulldog of obligations . . . a very mud-turtle for holding on. It is the heaviest thing of its weight in the world. I had one once, and sometimes I used to feel, as it rested on my roof, deadening the rain that fell there, and absorbing the sunshine, that it would crush through the shingles and rafters and overwhelm me with its dull and persistent weight.[48]

While the weight of mortgage helped to drag down the best farmer, Grady went further, explaining that this was not the worst of the problem. As the Georgia farmers struggled to pay off their loans, the interest

---

[46]Harris, 164-65.
[47]Harris, 165.
[48]Harris, 166.

payments they made stayed not in the state, but went instead to money lenders in New York and Boston. If this practice continued, Grady warned, Southern farmers would end up like the Irish who live in "mud cabins" and have to "send every tithe of their earnings to deepen the purple luxury of London."

In order to solve the worsening problem for the South's farmers, Grady offered specific advice for his audience. First, he recommended that farmers should not turn to the government because it was in the "hands of a party that was in sympathy with their oppressors." After providing examples of how the Republican Party was indeed the "apologists of the plutocrats" and based their power on increasing centralization in government, Grady stressed that this party also had the weight and power of a million and a half pensioners from the military to care for and look to for support. In order to deal with this "looting of the treasury," Grady urged his listeners to "stand upright among the states of this republic and declare her mind and stand by her convictions." If farmers would only voice their opinions, then

> the great American heart will burst with righteous wrath, and the voice of the people, which is the voice of God, will challenge the traitors, and the great masses will rise in their might, and breaking down the defenses of the oligarchs, will hurl them from power and restore the republic to the old moorings from which it had been swept by the storm.[49]

Grady ended his speech before the farmers of Elberton, Georgia, by "confessing" that the intensity of the struggle he outlined caused him to "grow faint." The political fight would not be easy, but if farmers would only "buckle on your armour, gird about your loins," and "stand upright and dauntless," then all would "prevail for liberty and truth."

Grady's Final Speeches

The themes articulated by Grady in his Elberton speech formed the pattern for a "dozen talks" which he made over a period of two months to audiences composed mostly of farmers. As economic conditions

---

[49]Harris, 175.

worsened, Grady feared that Southern farmers would turn to the Farmer's Alliance and effectively divide the white voters in the South. The editor had warned in his Dallas speech that this political division among Southern white voters would only "invite the debauching bid of factions" for the black voters. In Grady's vision, the results of this political infighting would result in Republican victory and the continuation of economic policies that would hurt both Southern whites and blacks.

On December 3, 1889, Henry Cabot Lodge, a Republican leader in the Senate, introduced a "Force Bill" calling for Federal protection of voting rights in the Southern states.[50] Grady had long feared this action, and, on December 12, he addressed the annual meeting of the Boston Merchant's Association, with race relations in the South as his theme.

Grady began his Boston speech by emphasizing that he stood to reiterate "every word" uttered in his New South address years ago in New York. Since the sentiments he had expressed in the New South speech were now "universally approved in the South," Grady moved on to stress that Southerners were assembling "a system of industries" that would "dazzle the world." But, in the midst of this new industrialization, Grady observed that the problem of the former slave still needed to be resolved.

As he had pointed out in Dallas, Grady told his Boston audience of the inherent inferiority of the Negro:

> Two utterly dissimilar races on the same soil—with equal political and civil right—almost equal in numbers, but terribly unequal in intelligence and responsibility—each pledged against fusion[51]

Since this race relations problem was an enormous issue to resolve, Grady appealed to his Northern listeners not to misjudge the reported acts of violence against Negroes. If such actions did occur, Grady argued that Southern society, "sentient and responsible in every fibre, can mend and repair until the whole has the strength of the best."

In response to the key question, "when could blacks cast a free ballot," Grady responded that Negroes could vote when they would no longer be under the "prey of the cunning and unscrupulous of both parties." Grady asked his Northern audience for five things:

---

[50]See Nixon, 316-17; and Bartley, 92.
[51]Harris, 18; See also the *Boston Evening Transcript*, 13 December 1889, 1-2.

First, patience; out of this alone can come perfect work. Second, confidence; this alone you can judge fairly. Third, sympathy; in this you can help best. Fourth, give us your sons as hostages. When you plant your capital in millions, send your sons that they may know how true are our hearts and may help swell the Anglo-Saxon current until it can carry without danger this infusion. Fifth, loyalty to the republic—for there is sectionalism in loyalty as in estrangement.[52]

Except for this passage, Grady's Merchant Association speech lacked the energy and intensity found in his other major speeches. The reason for this was Grady's poor state of health. He had suffered dizzy spells before taking the long train ride to Boston. During his stay in the North, Grady developed a very bad cold, but this illness did not keep him from delivering a final speech in Boston before the Bay State Club a few days later.

Grady began this final short speech with an acknowledgement that former President Grover Cleveland was in the audience. As he had mentioned in earlier speeches, the editor stressed that the important struggle being fought out in the country was "against the consolidation of power, the concentration of capital, the diminution of local sovereignty and the dwarfing of the individual citizen."[53] While Grady complimented President Cleveland for his efforts to act upon democratic principles, the Georgian emphasized that Southerners would not sacrifice their traditions, independence and regional pride. Grady concluded his Bay State Club speech by contending that:

We aim to make our homes, poor as they are, self-respecting and independent. We try to make them temples of refinement, in which our daughters may learn that woman's best charm and strength is her gentleness and her grace, and temples of liberty in which our sons may learn that no power can justify and no treason repay for the surrender of the slightest right of a free individual American citizen.[54]

Henry Grady returned to Atlanta on Monday, December 16, but was so ill that he had to be assisted from the train. Sometime during his return trip from Boston, Grady's cold developed into pneumonia, and his

---

[52]Harris, 197.
[53]Harris, 201.
[54]Harris, 203.

condition worsened as Christmas approached. On December 23, Grady died at the age of 39.

Grady's Metaphors: The Vision Unified

Beginning with his New South speech, Henry Grady's metaphors provided a powerful sense of direction for what the typical white Southerner's economic and cultural future should have been from the mid-1880s onward. Although the eloquent editor believed he could speak on behalf of his entire native region, most of Grady's metaphors generated a vision of "newness" for very selected audiences.

In the New South speech, Grady's intent was to begin the restructuring of the common associations of the typical Southerner in the mind of a wealthy Northern audience. The metaphors indicating the God-ordained birth of a new being on traditional Southern soil was necessary to reassure New York investors that the lazy "Cavalier" image of the Southerner had been forever transformed by the war. This new Southern creation held no bitterness toward the North and was, above all else, ready to put "business above politics." The only potential problem with a possible business arrangement between the North and the South was answered by Grady's attempt to show that the former slaves were now protected by the law and were also well-treated. The legal associations surrounding the Negro's status in the South was bluntly stated by Grady, but his metaphors on the future social standing of these former slaves were vague. Grady concluded the New South speech with the emotional appeal to Northerners to accept the reborn Southerner as a good financial investment and to be less concerned with the status of the Negro.

The most complete articulation of Grady's vision for racial relations in the South came from the metaphors in his Dallas speech. In this very long address, Grady's metaphors most clearly reveal his thinking about the future for the Southern white male. In the aftermath of the Civil War, he envisioned a new Southern creation, one whose blood was formulated by God to forever dominate the black race. This declaration, as the editor noted at the time, was no new truth. Instead of offering a new view on race relations, Grady sought to reassure his Southern audience that a new place for whites had now been heavenly prepared to assume on the newly vital Southern soil. Blacks, because of their inherently lower status, would remain manual laborers on the farms, while the former white "soldier-farmer" took his new place in an industrialized world of

Southern cities. In this mental picture of a new earthly marketplace, the white Southern industrialist would take his place with his Northern counterparts on the road to economic prosperity.

As economic conditions in the rural South worsened in the late 1880s, Henry Grady came to believe that only a financial and political union with the industrialized North would save the South. Starting with his New South speech, Grady attempted to rhetorically demonstrate the similarities between the Northern Puritan and the Southern Cavalier. After drawing the close metaphorical relationship between North and South, Grady hoped to find a new common ground for unity and dialogue between the two different regions. Since the Civil War and Reconstruction had forced the North and South together politically, Grady urged the Southerner to include "patriotism" as the key label of unity in the new vocabulary of dialogue with the North.

In Grady's Dallas speech, the common ground between the regions was further emphasized and extended by metaphors. The new creation emerging from the New South speech was shown to be able to think and act just like its Northern counterpart. Metaphorically, Grady vigorously asserted the economic similarities between the "soldier-farmer" and the "merchant." Without a trace of regional bitterness to hold them back, Grady demonstrated how the symbolic blood and courage of the Southern farmer-soldier was especially suitable for taking on a new role of financial cooperation with his Northern brothers to be merchants to the whole world.

In his University of Virginia and Elberton speeches, Grady assured Southern farmers that even if they chose not to leave agriculture, they could still have an honorable place in the new unified economic order. He tried to demonstrate that scientific advancement in industry would have corresponding benefits for farmers. Grady used metaphors of partnership and brotherhood to argue that farmers and science-inspired industry had common interests and goals. If Southern farmers somehow felt separated from the economic growth being forged by science, then Grady attached blame metaphorically to a Republican-inspired plot to centralize government only for the benefit of a select few. Grady ultimately urged Southern farmers, who traditionally associated their goals as similar to the Democrats, to stick with their party and eventually the benefits of science and mechanization would unite them in harmony with the new industrial order. Any effort on the part of farmers to join a movement to fight government centralization without the Democratic Party, Grady finally warned, would only allow the Negro to join ranks with the Republicans and make economic matters worse.

Grady's last speeches in Boston completed the rhetorical effort to avoid the dangers associated with political and economic disunity between North and South. He feared the enactment of a "force bill" by Northern Senators and the certain reduction in economic investment that the legislation would cause. Beyond this issue, however, Grady seemed to have feared a symbolic split in the Southern branch of the Democratic Party. Grady employed metaphors suggesting the common ground and goals between North and South in the hope to bring about a new economic and political dependency between the regions. He wanted to metaphorically depict to a Northern audience that the formerly isolated white Southerner was symbolically recreating himself in an industrial mind-set and thus the South was ripe for economic investment. But Grady's metaphorical transformation left little room in the post-Reconstruction South for blacks or poor white farmers who were either unwilling or unable to turn their rural communities into industrial meccas.

Grady's rhetorical assaults against Republicans and centralized government were metaphorically effective for a large group of middle class Southerners. The details, however, of just how science, patriotism, and the Democratic Party were to help poor white farmers fight the powerful economic forces allied against them was never made clear by Grady. While these Southern farmers were politically inactive and therefore patiently waiting their turn for advancement in the 1880s, Grady's assertion that they would share in the same progress as merchants in the cities offered little immediate comfort. Into the rhetorical vacuum of Grady's distant vision for Southern farmers moved the equally metaphorically-charged speeches of Thomas E. Watson.

Chapter 3

Tom Watson's Vision

"I saw from the address of Mr. Watson the prophecy of a great career in the use of the English language. His splendid diction, his brilliant thoughts, his deep pathos, showed me that he was a master of eloquence and I felt like Walter Scott after he had read Childe Harold, 'There is a master mind coming to the front'."

—Nathaniel E. Harris
Autobiography

Athens and Thomson are geographically located in Georgia's Piedmont region. This area of the state was well known for its fine cotton farming and political independence. Tom Watson dearly loved his home and displayed this great affection for his "home place" in the autobiographical novel, *Bethany: A Story of the Old South* (1904). After his father suffered great financial losses in the national economic recession of 1873-1874, Watson was unable to complete his studies at Mercer and returned to the family farm near Thomson. Forced to reenter the decimated agricultural community of rural Georgia, Watson knew firsthand the problems facing the Southern farmer, and, through metaphorical rhetoric, he worked to overcome them.

This chapter will outline Watson's early struggle to make a name for himself as a country lawyer and will review his major speeches prior to 1890 with a special emphasis on his metaphors as they appeared in important junctures in these speeches. The chapter will conclude with a critique of what Watson's metaphors suggested about his vision for the South's future at the end of the 1880s.

Watson Matures as Attorney and Speaker

Thomas E. Watson received his license to practice law on October 19, 1875. The Clerk of the Court in Richmond County, Georgia, issued the license on credit since Watson was unable to pay the fee at the time. Leaving Augusta almost immediately, Watson returned to Screven County to begin his legal career. During his first year of practice, Watson taught school partime in order to supplement his meager case load. The rural, agricultural communities of Screven deeply impressed Watson; he wrote: "I think that my earnest sympathy for the poor dates from this period of my life." But, due to financial concerns, Watson left Screven County within a year for the town of Thomson.[1]

After appealing to one of his old teachers in Thomson, R. H. Pearce, Watson was advanced room and board until he could establish his new practice. He supplemented his income by assisting the McDuffie County Clerk in recording deeds, mortgages, and other important documents. His first year of law practice yielded a gross income of $212.[2]

While Watson struggled to build his law practice in the late 1870s, he often found himself with extra time on his hands. In order to fight off boredom, Watson used some of his lonely hours to write poetry. Eventually Watson persuaded the *McDuffie Journal* to publish two of his poems "celebrating the genuine romance of Napoleon Bonaparte and Josephine Beauharnais."[3]

During Watson's second full year as a practicing attorney, he bought back on credit one of the old "home places" near Thomson that had belonged to his family. After moving his father, mother, brothers, and sisters from Augusta into their old home, Watson supported them with his growing practice. Every morning, Watson would leave home with his dinner tin and walk the three miles to his office in Thomson. Although his legal fees were often small, Watson's fame as a criminal attorney quickly spread around the local area. The young Watson would take

---

[1]C. Vann Woodward, *Tom Watson: Agrarian Rebel* (London: Oxford University Press, 1938) 35.

[2]Thomas E. Watson, *Life and Speeches* (Nashville: The Author, 1908) 13.

[3]As cited in William W. Brewton, *The Life of Thomas E. Watson* (Atlanta: The Author, 1926) 96-97.

almost any case, but, because civil cases took much time in "studied preparation, he often declined these in favor of criminal cases he could argue in front of a jury."[4] It was in front of a twelve-member jury that Watson honed his oratorical skills. Since Watson grew up in the four-county area around Thomson where he practiced, he could easily adapt his forensic rhetoric into the "rural idiom" and win over even the most skeptical juror. Between 1877 and 1880, Watson rarely lost a criminal case. During this time, it became a widely prevalent belief that there was an "agreement of honor" in the area where Watson practiced that he would not assist in the prosecution of one charged with murder, for if he did, it meant certain death for the defendant.[5] Watson reserved his talent in forensic rhetoric for the defense. By the end of his third full year of legal practice, Watson's income had grown to over $12,000 per year.[6]

As Watson's fame as a criminal attorney grew, he began receiving numerous invitations to speak at ceremonial occasions. During the late spring, Watson's favorite occasion to deliver a speech was during the commencement exercises of local county "academies."[7] One of his first commencement addresses was presented before Professor W. C. Reynold's Academy at Union Point, Georgia in the spring of 1878. In this speech, Watson offered some advice to the graduates as to how they could improve conditions throughout the South.

Watson first emphasized to his young audience that he wanted them to help him "win back the empire you had to lose." The metaphors used by Watson to describe the South's future "empire" are revealing:

we want to crown the old red hills of Georgia once more with happy homes and firesides, while the hum of the mill and factory shall mingle with the riffle of her dreamlets.[8]

Though Watson's view of the South's future was not yet complete, he was certain as to the kind of vision that must be avoided by Southerners. Watson argued:

---

[4]Brewton, 135-36.
[5]Woodward, *Tom Watson*, 51.
[6]Watson, *Life and Speeches*, 13.
[7]Brewton, 141.
[8]Thomas E. Watson Papers, Southern Historical Collection, University of North Carolina at Chapel Hill, *Journal #2*, 247.

> We have grown sick of failures. Merchants fail and their creditors with
> solemn consternation flock to the bankrupt court to see if they can get
> ten cents on the dollar. Farmers fail . . . and commission men vulture-
> like, come swooping in with their mortgage waivers and the horses are
> knocked off under; and the old homestead, endeared and sanctified by
> a thousand tender memories passes into the lordship of strangers.[9]

In these vivid examples, Watson urged his young listeners to succeed
and, above all, to avoid the "misfortunes of the past." Their efforts would
not be easy, Watson observed, because "our cities are frustrated, and our
industries paralyzed."

A few months after delivering the Union Point commencement address, Watson was invited to speak before the Thomson "Gallispaen Society." In this short ceremonial address, Watson's metaphors revealed more
of his thinking about the South's future. He began the speech by paying
homage to "Gallisope," the Goddess of Eloquence that "was worshipped
ages ago in the Isles of Greece." After further paying respects to "genius"
and "literature," he stressed how these two divine forces combine to create eloquence. He defined the power of eloquence as: "What the wind is
to the waves, what the moon is to the tides, eloquence is to Man."[10]

As an example of the effectiveness of eloquence in the South, Watson explained that the Southern ear still felt the vibrations of Robert
Toombs's pre-Civil War oratory. Concerning Toombs's contribution to
the war, Watson asserted that:

> The southern heart is on fire from his blazing appeals. The warriors
> came, "as the clans of Roderick woke the highland." The southern flags
> flushed to the front. And a hundred battlefields can scarcely quench in
> blood the flames which one man's eloquence had mainly kindled.[11]

These passages demonstrate that Watson was not only thinking about
the future of his homeland, but how his own oratory might someday
make a difference. In a section of his personal journal, Watson pondered
the "fate of reformers." He defined "reform" as the "spirit, pure and hea-
ven-born, which soars above the things of corruption and reveals in the

---

[9]Watson Papers, *Journal #2*, 248.
[10]Watson Papers, *Journal #2*, 258-59.
[11]Watson Papers, *Journal #2*, 259.

pure ether of truth or holiness." Watson was realistic about the many difficulties of reform efforts:

> He who undertakes to reform mankind condemns himself to a herculean task. Men have a morbid dislike of change. They cling with affection to customs of their fathers and the reformer who introduces a practical, philosophical, or religious change is met with bitter persecution.[12]

In spite of the personal struggles involved with leading a life of reform, Watson believed that the new age he lived in demanded activism. After outlining the personal problems faced by reformers, Watson noted:

> Most emphatically, this is an age of progress. Discoveries, aided by the energy of enterprise have wrought a change in the very aspect of the world. Old institutions have been supplanted. Old forms have been abolished. The current of events has washed away nearly all the landmarks of the past and is sweeping onward into the untrodden realities of the future. Onward is the watchword of the times.[13]

These early speeches and journal entries reveal a time of great introspection for the young attorney. His metaphors indicate that he recognized the power of rhetoric to generate concern for the improvement of Southern society. Watson's rhetoric also reveals that he had not yet organized his own thoughts into a fully coherent vision of the South's future.

As the 1880s dawned, Watson continued to deliver ceremonial speeches in front of almost any audience that would invite him. On July 28, 1880, Watson addressed the graduating class at Mercer High School in Penfield, Georgia. In this speech, the tone of the reformer began to assert itself through Watson's metaphors. Since the audience consisted primarily of local farmers, Watson's thesis on how agriculture might achieve "Victory" in this new age was appropriate.

Watson began the Penfield speech by recognizing that the Southern farmer had been "looking anxiously" for the time "when his barns shall be filled, his acres extended, uneasiness driven from his door, and he shall rule independently in his cottage home." These hopeful expectations, however, were not coming to pass. Watson noted that farmers

---

[12]Watson Papers, *Journal #2*, 102.
[13]Watson Papers, *Journal #2*, 102.

faced hardships because of low prices, high mortgages and insensitive merchants. These formidable obstacles to farmers had to be removed—only then could they be "independent lords of the soil and not the slaves of commissioners, merchants, and cotton factors."

According to Watson, Southern farmers could rightfully blame their troubles on the "traders of the East who were looking for an easy highway into the market of the world." While the market for Southern cotton expanded, the small farmer was not receiving the benefits. Watson argued:

> I have seen that the showers of gold which fall from the South in return for her cotton find its way into the pockets of men who never ran the cotton fields, while the laborer who did it all . . . rage from one end of the year to the other.[14]

Extending the metaphorical "Lords of the soil" into part of his solution for the farmer's problem, Watson warned that, in the future, laborers, conscious of their "first reward," would rise up and say: "Give us our rights." Once this battle had been joined, to the victors belonged a "banquet hall laden down with tempting honors." Large Northern banks would be forced to make more capital available to needy Southern farmers.

As Watson concluded his speech at Mercer High School, he cautioned his listeners that their battle would not necessarily be won under current economic conditions. He ended the speech by urging the laborers of Penfield to be more "like Spartacus; if we must die, let us die by the bright waters under the clear skies in noble honorable battle."

The warfare metaphors used by Watson in his Penfield speech suggest that he had devoted much of his thinking to how to reform the current economic and social conditions that poor Southerners faced. Although a full description of the evil facing farmers was not yet made clear, Watson's identification of the Southern farmer as a "laborer" was a significant metaphorical transition. Since the economic conditions of the day did not permit farmers to quickly acquire wealth, their role in the economic order was not assured, and therefore they would have to fight for their financial prosperity.

In November 1892, Watson was easily elected to the lower house of the Georgia General Assembly. This political victory was a natural

---

[14]Watson Papers, *Journal #2*, 268.

stepping stone for a young, ambitious attorney of the day. As a Democrat in a rural farm district, Watson quickly out-distanced all his other white opponents to win the election by a majority of 392 votes.[15]

As a newly-elected legislator, Watson quickly established a reputation as a reformer. His first victory was the elimination of the convict lease system which rural county commissioners frequently abused. Watson argued that the system "commercialized the state's sovereign right to punish her criminals to money-making companies whose only interest was to maintain the convict at the lowest possible cost and to work him at the utmost human capacity."[16] Watson also attempted to pass legislation safeguarding the belongings of tenant farmers in the event of litigation from landowners. This bill to help farmers failed, and Watson suffered further defeats through the rest of his short term. In his private journal, Watson noted that he "found no pleasure in the legislature and was not satisfied with" his share of legislation.

Before leaving the Georgia legislature, Watson was called upon to deliver one of his most widely distributed ceremonial speeches.[17] On March 4, 1882, Alexander H. Stephens, the former vice-president of the Confederacy and then current Georgia governor, died. In honor of Stephens, Watson delivered one of the many eulogies to this former Confederate leader. In the epideictic or ceremonial address, Watson continued his metaphorical references to warrior figures by observing that:

> With Mr. Stephens the contest is over. He had gone out in the serried ranks of life; he had borne him like a true knight, without fear and without reproach. . . . The great commander has sounded the recall, and this veteran was on his return, with the laurel upon his brow, the olive leafe in his hand, victory upon his head, and peace in his heart.[18]

Watson's metaphor describing God as a "great commander" was one of the most interesting features of the Stephens eulogy. The early speeches by Watson suggested visions of stormy controversy in the South's future. With his various Warrior metaphors, Watson helped to identify the figures to be involved in the growing social and economic conflict. As

---

[15]Woodward, *Tom Watson*, 102.
[16]As cited by Woodward, *Tom Watson*, 105-106.
[17]Brewton, 180-81.
[18]As cited by Brewton, 182-83.

a great commander, God was more than a merely concerned observer of the impeding battle. Southern farmers had to begin preparing for a new struggle against earthly enemies. God could be on the farmer's side, but only if the proper "heroic" lessons were learned from past leaders such as Stephens. While these images seemed to have dominated Watson's thinking about the future of the South, it was only after he left the Georgia legislature that he began to deliver his most culturally significant discourses.

The Mature Epideictic: Watson's Speeches, 1883-1886

The Fourth of July celebration in the South, as in other regions of the country, developed into a grand event often lasting several days. The high point of this occasion was the delivery of a Fourth of July oration by an important speaker of the day.[19] On July 4, 1883, Watson delivered the main address at the celebration in Greensboro, Georgia.

Watson told his mostly rural audience at Greensboro that he would speak of the South and her welfare. After recounting the shattered and devastated condition of the South after the war, Watson launched into an extended metaphorical assessment of why Southerners should not dwell too long over past losses. Watson argued:

> he who would seek to vent his grief over the past would find an empty tomb . . . saying "why seek ye the living among the dead? She is not here but risen!" From under the shroud she pulsates back to life; over death, a conqueror over the grave, a victor she has gone to the glories of the future chastened and purified by the baptism of the blood.[20]

Combined with this vision of a symbolic resurrection, Watson indicated in his metaphors of a transition from the past to the present. In this speech, Watson's stormy sea vision of societal conflict was best demonstrated:

---

[19]See, for example, Howard H. Martin, "The Fourth of July Oration," *Quarterly Journal of Speech* 44 (December 1958): 393-401.

[20]Watson Papers, *Journal #2*, 318.

the deluge has been great and many of the things we loved have been swept away by its waters. But the Dove has come back to the Ark—the olive leaf she bears is fresh of green—and hope the divine . . . may yet be won.[21]

These passages provide evidence of Watson's awareness that a great economic and social transition was underway in the South. He believed, however, that the Georgia farmer should enjoy the new time of peace as he had in antebellum times. In order for the Southern farmer to make the adjustments necessary to be successful in this new peacetime, Watson recommended a renewal of the importance of self-sufficiency. He noted that the South had:

waterflows to speed the machinery of the world. We have mines rich with every precious ore . . . we have a soil capable of feeding every citizen of America.[22]

Even with these abundant natural resources, Watson pointed out the contradiction of the South having to buy cloth from New England, grain from the West, meat from the Midwest, and milk from the Southwest. Watson asserted that these economic paradoxes were due to a "perfect mania for buying." Unless the Southerner relieved himself of this "senseless craze," Watson warned that the rebuilding region would lose not only its money, but its "natural advantage" as well.

In order for the South to once again assume a sense of economic sovereignty, Watson recognized the need for outside capital. This external funding, however, should not be sought at the expense of Southern honor. On this point, Watson's metaphors were very explicit:

Let us learn our lesson while we may and stop the leaks before the vessel sinks. Let our own markets supply our wants and our resources be developed. Let us stop this eternal leaning upon someone else.[23]

Watson's plan for restoring honor to the Southern economy contained three basic elements. First, Northern bankers would need to recognize the special problems of Southern farmers and supply them capital at lower

---

[21]Watson Papers, *Journal #2*, 318.
[22]Watson Papers, *Journal #2*, 319.
[23]Watson Papers, *Journal #2*, 321.

interest rates than the high "illegal ones" currently available. Second, cotton commissioners in the North and South must "obey the law" and provide adequate prices for Southern crops. Finally, Watson saved his most vivid metaphors for describing the evils of the present tariff system that needed to be abolished in order to truly help the Southern farmer compete with the rest of the world. Called a "Fortified Wall" that was "built to keep off foreign trade in order that homemade goods may command their own price," Watson stated that this form of "robbery" forced farmers to pay more for their supplies while receiving less for their crops traded on foreign markets. In some cases, foreign markets retaliated against the Southern farmer by completely closing their markets to them because of the high tariffs imposed on foreign-made consumer goods when they entered the United States. In order to correct this economic injustice caused by Northern industrialists who did not care what happened to farmers, Watson's plan was simple:

> Give us the freedom of making our own bargains. Make the consumer
> the equal of the producer and in the name of the God of justice, strip
> not the poor to pamper the rich.[24]

A final recommendation to the Greensboro audience was to improve the educational system in the South. Watson noted that Southern schools were in a very "unsatisfactory state" and unless the South built more schools immediately, they would have to build more jails later. Watson concluded his speech with the plea to improve education, but he added that students must be "educated with moral training" as well.

Watson's emphasis on Southern honor, self-sufficiency, and morality helped to clarify his metaphorical vision of the future for his rural audience. Although he softened his use of military metaphors, Watson's continued usage of stormy figures of speech suggested his persistent concern with political and economic reform amidst existing social turmoil. Like Grady, Watson realized that the South was experiencing great change. The new age would require some patience, but Watson's rhetoric suggests some growing bitterness at the economic unfairness of the system. Southern farmers, in Watson's view, were battling forces far beyond their control. In addition, farmers were being asked to share too much of these great burdens of economic growth. Watson rhetorically reached out

---

[24]Watson Papers, *Journal #2*, 326.

to offer not only a sympathetic ear, but to offer optimism—a truly hopeful vision.

On June 29, 1886, Watson returned to his alma mater Mercer University to deliver the commencement address.[25] As one of the longest ceremonial speeches Watson had presented up to that time, he used the occasion to expand upon the proper theme that Southerners should be concerned about for their future. The key problem that the South faced, according to Watson, was the "spread of an empire of disbelief—an empire which preserves no temples sacred from attack."[26] This growing sense of cynicism and skepticism was marked by a lack of "respect for character, no reverence for anything past or present, human or divine." Watson proposed to explain to his Mercer audience how this new creed of "narrow, unsympathizing selfishness" threatened the South's future.

Watson made it clear at the outset of his speech that he respected the type of skepticism that led individuals to "fairly investigate and intelligently decide." Instead of this healthy analytical approach, however, Watson warned his audience that the "new skeptic" questioned the honor of the past and casts the future in the "color green." Since "green was the color of the glasses" of this new skeptic, "all he sees is green." In Watson's critique of this new creed, he pondered the consequences of having "all things selling for a price." The result:

men have sold their convictions—their country—their kings—their God. . . . the circasian will sell his son for the army—his daughter for the harem . . . the soldier will sell his valor and his blood—the priest his prayers and absolution—the patriot the cause for which he bleeds.[27]

Since the new skeptic cares nothing for honor or respect, the lust for money became a power to fear in Watson's vision. His metaphors were exceptionally harsh, but he did not let up in his assessment of the darkening gloom settling over the South. Watson further observed that followers of this new creed were easy to identify because:

---

[25]The date is verified in the Watson Papers, *Journal #2*, 378. A complete text of the speech is also available in Thomas E. Watson, *The Life and Speeches of Thomas E. Watson* (Nashville: The Author, 1908) 41-58.

[26]Watson, *Life and Speeches*, 41.

[27]Watson, *Life and Speeches*, 43.

The belief is a faithful mirror to those who embrace it—to men who believe evilly because too often they seek an evil creed to fit an evil life. They get the idea that the world is a sea where the big fish eat the little fish and that the only way to escape being devoured is to devour all others, and grasping, therefore, they must snatch. All others cheat, therefore they must swindle.[28]

These metaphors, cast in Watson's typical stormy sea tone, were clear warnings against a rush into competitive industrialization. Watson feared the decline of old Southern values and the eventual rise of a brutal, consuming environment where any kind of weakness would draw attack from stronger foes. In blunt language, Watson stated that he "denied and scorned" this new creed. He lamented to the Mercer audience that he could not personally "stamp this out from the face of the earth."

In order to counter the rise of the skeptic's creed, Watson pleaded with his listeners to return to the old principles of manhood: "kindness, truth, honor, and loyalty." The central value that Watson expanded upon was the significance of truth to culture. He argued that:

truth is the basis of the fame of painter, and sculptor, orator and poet, statesman and philosopher: that institutions and laws, principles and creeds, die, with the day or outlive the centuries just in proportion as they conform to or are opposed by the resistless power of truth.[29]

As a way of sharpening the comparisons and irony in a world without truth or faith in personal honesty, Watson pointed out that the vast fortunes of the Rothchilds depended on respect and trust. If the new creed of disbelief became dominant, Watson contended that the business of mankind would come to a halt:

The great loom of traffic weaves no more. The great ocean of commerce checks its currents, calls in its tides, and a Dead Sea is before you; and around us, in place of town and village and city, is the silence and emptiness of the desert. Your Black Fridays come—your panics of '73 with the terror of the cyclone and the rumbling of an earthquake. The markets of the world tremble and smite their knees in abject dismay. Commercial houses topple, banks crash, values shrink,

---

[28]Watson, *Life and Speeches*, 44.
[29]Watson, *Life and Speeches*, 48-49.

securities vanish, stocks melt and through the gloom come the cries of distress from me and women and children.[30]

Using the metaphorical tone of a prophet, Watson's warnings blended the harsh personal examples of the past and projected, in stark contrast, an even more horrible future. If truth and honesty declined and all things in one's life are assigned a price, then the cycle of competition and betrayal would result in terrible personal hardships for rich and poor alike. The Watson vision recommended a renewal of the old principles of truth and loyalty that "build up rather than tear down and praise rather than slander."

In Watson's conclusion, he recognized the skepticism that might exist in his audience about the simple solution he offered—to cling to truth. He argued that it was not always easy to be scorned for being on the "losing side," but Watson reminded his listeners that true honor would only come to those who "stand erect in the plentitude of a royal manliness and think and believe and speak and act by the grand old principles of right." Finally, Watson offered Robert E. Lee as the ideal example of standing by truth.

The symbolic use of Robert E. Lee in Watson's commencement speech at Mercer is very significant rhetorically. As a ceremonial speech, the commencement address falls into the genre of epideictic discourse. Aristotle believed that this special specie of rhetoric had as its objective "to get the audience to view the person or action in question as honorable."[31] In addition, the speaker delivering an epideictic oration usually assumes the role as an "educator" to his or her audience because specific virtues of the deceased are praised for all in the community to emulate."[32]

Robert E. Lee had died on October 12, 1870. Since this time, Southern orators had praised the fallen general as the "sacred symbol" of the Old South.[33] By evoking Lee's image, Watson sought to encourage his

---

[30]Watson, *Life and Speeches*, 50-51.

[31]George A. Kennedy, *Classical Rhetoric and its Christian and Secular Tradition from Ancient to Modern Times* (Chapel Hill: University of North Carolina Press, 1980) 74.

[32]See C. H. Perelman and L. Olsbrechts-Tyteca, *The New Rhetoric: A Treatise on Argumentation*, trans. Purcell Weaver and John Wilkinson (South Bend: University of Notre Dame Press, 1969) 51.

[33]See, for example, Hal W. Fulmer, "Southern Clerics and the Passing of Lee: Mythic Rhetoric and the Construction of a Sacred Symbol," *Southern Communication*

audience not to completely abandon the "old" values of the South. Since Grady referred to Lincoln in his New South speech before a New York audience, Watson's use of Lee with a Southern audience provided an important contrast in rhetorical strategy between the two orators. Abraham Lincoln was a "national" symbol that Grady used to demonstrate how willing the South was to fully unite symbolically with the North. Watson warned his Macon audience to stand by the true virtues depicted in the life and values of Lee as a regional symbol of solidarity. The image of Lee became an important "mental bridge" for Southerners as they pondered the appropriate heroic role model that could best fire their imaginations into the uncertain future.[34]

An Aggressive Epideictic: Watson's Speeches, 1888-1889

Watson's ceremonial speeches through 1887 displayed a strong concern for the traditional social and economic systems of the South. His metaphors urged a renewed consideration for regional economic sovereignty and warned against financial dependency on Northern bankers. Watson also worried aloud to his rural audiences about a shift in values away from personal honor and loyalty to the traditional Southern creed. The Watson vision contained metaphorical warnings against a shift toward an ideological creed of materialism and selfish greed. Except for a short term as a state legislator, Watson avoided politics up through 1887. Between 1880 and 1887, his ceremonial speeches were directed at rural Southern audiences in the tone of a concerned prophet. In 1888, however, Watson's public dialogue began to take on a different rhetorical focus.

Since 1888 was an important election year, Watson left his law practice and became a candidate for elector at large for the state Democratic ticket. As a loyal Democrat, Watson stumped the state for Grover Cleveland, but made tariff reform a special issue of his campaign.[35] Just before

---

Journal 55 (Summer 1990) 355-71.

[34]For a more complete discussion of the cultural role that symbolic memorials of fallen Confederate leaders played during the 1880s, please see George M. Foster, *Ghosts of the Confederacy: Defeat, the Lost Cause, and the Emergence of the New South 1865 to 1913* (New York: Oxford University Press, 1987): 88-103.

[35]Watson, *Life and Speeches*, 14.

the campaign formally began in August, Watson accepted an invitation to address the graduating class of Milledgeville Academy in Milledgeville, Georgia in June of 1888.[36] The city of Milledgeville had once been the capital of the state, so it was an appropriate setting for a speech with strong political overtones.

Watson introduced his thesis to the Milledgeville audience through an extended allegory. Asking his listeners to recall a scene in a recently released novel, Watson described how even in the total desolation of a city, a "Temple of Truth still stood." In the midst of the silence surrounding the Temple, a veiled female statue remained unharmed. Through the shadow of moonlight, Watson read the statue's inscription for the audience: "Truth beseeching the world to lift her veil."

After asking the graduates to accept "Truth" as his thesis, Watson proposed to explain just how imperishable this ideal really was for the world. He advised them that the pursuit of truth is the "highest purpose which man can have in his life." While additional creeds could live or die, Watson asserted that truth provided the strongest "constant tendency in the universe."

The first example provided by Watson of those who correctly sought the truth was the philosopher. He observed that the world owed a great gratitude to philosophers because they:

robbed the eclipse of the terror which once sent the nations to their knees; severed famine and pestilence and earthquake from any connection from the wrath of God; established the uniformity and permanency of nature's laws, and hurled superstition from the throne in the minds and hearts of men.[37]

Besides the philosopher, Watson noted that the statesman had long been assigned the task of writing the law "in conformity with truth." Starting with Moses, Watson demonstrated that the statesman had tried to find the "true relation between innocence and guilt, between crime and punishment." He pointed out that while lawmakers have truth as a goal,

---

[36]The best text of this speech is in Watson, *Life and Speeches*, 59-73. An identical text of the Milledgeville address also appears in Vol. 9 of *History of Southern Oratory in the South in the Building of the Nation,* ed. Watson, 454-71. It should be noted that in Watson's *History of Southern Oratory* volume, the date for the speech is incorrectly listed as "1890."

[37]Watson, *Life and Speeches*, 60.

the legal code did not always speak the "truth upon all subjects." In fact, Watson lamented that in a court of law, he often felt compelled to:

> deface, disfigure, and demolish an honest witness to such an extent that his neighbors on the jury will forget that he is a reputable citizen who has sworn the truth.[38]

From alliterative examples such as these, Watson told his audience that "in God's name, are we not drifting away from the truth when our lands, liberty, and life may depend on the speech of an advocate?"

Since the South was moving further from truth and even listening to the false truths of Grady, Watson urged his own audience to consider reforms. Change was needed because the "public had lost confidence in the system." The specific harms to Southern farmers were reasons enough to seek alternatives to the present system. Watson said:

> A system which tears a white tenant from his family and puts him in chains and stripes because he sells cotton for something to eat and leaves his rent unpaid, and which at the same time cannot punish its railroad kings who shamelessly violate the penal statutes, is a system which no honest man can heartily respect.[39]

According to Watson, the central problem with the economic system was that it was "unequal in its treatment of the classes, the unequal levying of taxes, and the unequal distribution of wealth." These three main causes, he asserted, had helped to "people the cemeteries of the past with dead empires."

As an illustration of how history might change if the inequality between the classes were not addressed soon, Watson offered an extended example of how economic abuses caused the French Revolution. He further argued that in France the "abuses were so terrible" that some of the "fairest provinces" had their life "crushed out" and the countryside became a "desert while the cities were crowded with the starving peasants who had left them." When the poor finally had been taxed to the limit, Watson explained that the French King turned to tax the noblemen and they revolted causing the French Revolution.

---

[38]Watson, *Life and Speeches*, 63.
[39]Watson, *Life and Speeches*, 64.

After demonstrating how inequality between the classes brought down the French empire, Watson cautioned his audience not to depend on the equality guaranteed in the Declaration of Independence. In spite of the efforts of Thomas Jefferson to battle the forces of "class, special privilege, concentrated power and corporate wealth," Watson asserted that Alexander Hamilton and his followers had almost won their economic battle to create a "consolidated empire."

Though Hamilton's financial dream had nearly come true, Watson proclaimed that this "system is false and cannot live." He pointed out that this consolidated empire would be judged false in any court: the Declaration of Independence, the Constitution, or even the "Republican spirit of the people." As the central metaphor of evil, this "consolidated empire" vision was explored in great detail:

> the tendency of the government to favor some industries at the expense of others; to favor some classes at the expense of others; to enforce general contributions for all the people when the benefit goes directly into the pockets of a few; to grant special privileges to some which it denies to others; to place the taxes almost entirely upon those least able to bear them.[40]

Besides indicating the list of grievances of the poor against the government, Watson also emphasized one of the most destructive elements of the present economic system was the:

> aiding and encouraging the strong to oppress the weak—sanctioning the large fortune when it swallows the small one, and the large one when it gobbles up the large one; and fostering the trust which destroys or absorbs the independent enterprises that would stand against it.[41]

The metaphorical evils facing the young graduate were very oppressive, but Watson moved into a description of how a career choice might help solve the economic abuses of the system. Since Watson was an attorney, he first explained how those choosing law could make a difference in society. Noting that the "signal fires of the Revolution were lit," and the "Declaration of Independence, written by a lawyer," Watson held

---

[40]Watson, *Life and Speeches*, 66.
[41]Watson, *Life and Speeches*, 66.

up the image of Thomas Jefferson as the "true lawyer" for his commencement audience. Above all, Watson argued, Jefferson was a true "ornament of our profession and demonstrated its opportunities for good."

If the new graduates did not choose to be lawyers, Watson next explored the opportunities that might be available to them as politicians. Even though he had to admit that the political profession suffered from a terrible reputation, Watson told his listeners that politicians still had a noble mission in society:

> to denounce abuses and propose remedies; to oppose bad laws and to advocate new ones; to educate the masses of the people upon the true principles of government, to lead them in opposition of administrative wrongs; to embolden them to stand squarely for their guaranteed right, to labor to the end that equity shall be preserved, that the avenues of promotion shall be open to all alike, and that the country shall be henceforth and forever a decent place for the people to live in.[42]

After detailing what the "true politician" should have as his creed, Watson finally turned to a discussion of the farming profession. He admitted that it was unlikely that any new graduate would think about being a farmer because:

> There is no charm in agriculture now. The country mansions have gone to decay; the fields are worn to sand or seamed with gullies; the ditches in the low ground have filled, and the meadow, ah! the green, flower-scented meadow we children loved, has become a marsh.[43]

As Watson began to describe the decline of agriculture in the South, his metaphors revealed a strong emotional attachment for past traditions and institutions:

> . . . gone is the orchard with its snow-drift of apple blossoms, its aroma of velvet peach; and the spring at the foot of the hill, where the melon used to cool, is choked with weeds; and the path which leads to it has had no foot steps upon it this many a year.[44]

---

[42]Watson, *Life and Speeches*, 69.
[43]Watson, *Life and Speeches*, 70.
[44]Watson, *Life and Speeches*, 71.

The cause for this decline in Watson's beloved Southern farm life was simply stated: "there was a mortgage; there was a lawsuit; there was a sheriff's sale." After this quick chain of events, the "family broke up" and "moved to town." To answer the question of why the Southern farm family left the farm, Watson repeated some of his earlier list of charges against the system:

> The fact that it was well-nigh impossible to prosper in the country. The pitiless burden of equal taxation, the impossibility of buying or selling except at other people's prices. A currency system which made the farmer and his lands on outlaw from its benefits; these and causes similar to these broke his fortune and broke his spirit—took his farm and took his home.[45]

In order to restore hope to the farmer and his way of life, Watson urged his listeners to demand of their political rulers that "the law shall treat your industries as it treats other, equally as to burdens, equally as to benefits." Economic and spiritual equality must be established, and the Watson metaphors made clear connections to the glories of the South's agricultural past. He stressed that there "was no shame" in hoping that:

> the old folks would come back from town, reshingle the "big house" and reset the flower yard. I wish that I could see every parlor rehung with the family pictures, and the grass cleared away from the graves of those who sleep under the trees in the garden. Would that this country could be built up again, and built up by those who love it most.[46]

Watson concluded his Milledgeville commencement address by pleading with his audience to demand that their legislators "grant justice" to Southern farmers. As he ended the speech, Watson extolled his listeners to seek the truth about the farm crisis and specifically avoid the messages of newspaper editors. These Southern newspaper editors, Watson argued, had not actually "gone among these people and counted the wounded, the dying, and the dead, in the field where they fell." He believed that before any "big city" editor could lead public opinion to the truth, these writers must first go into the poor rural counties of Georgia and view for themselves the condition of the farmers on the land.

---

[45]Watson, *Life and Speeches*, 71.
[46]Watson, *Life and Speeches*, 72.

It can be inferred from the peroration of Watson's Milledgeville speech that he had several points of contention with the editor of the largest newspaper in Georgia, Henry W. Grady of the *Atlanta Constitution*. As the November 1888 election date neared, Watson began a speaking tour throughout the rural counties of south central Georgia. In three of these speeches, Watson directly attacked Grady by name and the "new creed" that the editor was advocating in his speeches and editorials.

On August 30, 1888, Watson addressed a military reunion in Lincolnton, Georgia. His speech on this occasion survives only in synopsis form, but Watson's key arguments come through clearly. After humorously recalling the stories he had heard as a child about "Hood flanking Sherman before Atlanta," Watson stressed that the hardships after the war welded a "Solid South" built on "common suffering" like those faced by the Israelites in the wilderness. For the future, Watson asserted that the Southerner's goals should be the "security of Home-life," and "purity of the judiciary and integrity of political affairs." This should be the proper creed, Watson concluded, in direct contrast to Grady's perspective. Concerning the alternative creed, Watson argued:

> have no patience with that sickly sentiment, promulgated by some people of the South who, while crying out "new South," were apologizing for the South, our fathers, and of the war. Such sycophancy was not the stuff of which the highest order of southern manhood was made. Nor does such truculency meet with any high encomiums even from the brave and gallant men of the north.[47]

Watson further explained to his Lincolnton veterans that they should have little respect for the speeches given by Grady outside the South. Watson declared: "[S]hame to southern men who go to northern men and glory in our defeat . . . Unpaternal! Parricidal!"[48]

Instead of the selfish, self-serving New South Creed offered by Grady, Watson pleaded with his listeners to:

---

[47]Watson Papers, *Journal #2*, 409.
[48]Watson Papers, *Journal #2*, 409.

Stand for the "Solid South." Solid in its reverence for traditions of our past—in its loyalty to home rule—to home government. Solid in its struggle against tariff robbery, class legislation—the greed and growth of monopoly.[49]

A few days after his Lincolnton address, Watson delivered a similar attack on Grady's philosophy in a speech in Warrenton, Georgia on October 3, 1888. The major theme of this speech was once again the importance of maintaining political solidarity throughout the rural South. Watson said:

I want to warn you that carelessness and indifference will bring a want of harmony and in the end ruin an enterprise, person or party, no matter how united and strong they once were.[50]

According to Watson, the major danger to political unity and social harmony in the South was Henry Grady and his followers. He argued that:

There are certain men in Congress and certain influential newspapers diametrically opposed to the sentiment which prevails almost unanimously throughout the South. And if seeds sown by these parties are not uprooted before they germinate and bring forth fruit, the results will be that the solid South . . . will be disrupted and ruin will follow to the Party.[51]

Unlike Grady, Watson viewed the Solid South metaphor as one that clearly included poor Democrats of all races. Watson used metaphors expressing friendship to indicate that the poor classes of the South, both black and white, should stay together in political battle. He concluded to his Warrenton audience that political division among the races would:

be the greatest calamity that could befall us. The solid South is the greatest blessing that every white man and every colored man who will go with us—and they will all go with us for we are their friends—ever enjoyed.[52]

---

[49]Watson Papers, *Journal #2*, 410.
[50]Watson Papers, *Journal #2*, 414.
[51]Watson Papers, *Journal #2*, 414.
[52]Watson Papers, *Journal #2*, 414.

The dominant metaphor to emerge from the Lincolnton and Warrenton speeches by Watson was the vision of a politically and spiritually unified or "solid" South of all the poor farmers in the region. Prior to 1888, Watson's stormy metaphors suggested his general displeasure with the present economic system. As the election of 1888 neared, Watson appealed broadly to his poor, rural audience to recognize their traditional common complaints against the system and stand together against any new economic creed that offered them little opportunity for self-improvement. Watson read many Georgia newspapers on a regular basis and was therefore well aware of Henry Grady's growing influence even among the poor counties around the state. The metaphors used by Watson in 1888 demonstrated that he objected to Grady's political motives and to the new economic order that the editor advocated.

Just a few days before the polls opened, Tom Watson addressed a large audience at the Georgia State Fair in Macon, Georgia, on November 8, 1888. Since this was his last opportunity to define his vision for the Georgia electorate, Watson used his most vivid metaphors to contrast his position with that of Henry Grady.

Watson began his Macon speech by recalling for his audience that the South's "grandest triumphs" had been "sanctified by the sacrifices of our martyrs." From this appeal to the fallen dead of the Civil War, Watson moved next to explain how some Democrats in the South had overlooked the obvious "bribery and treachery in New York" concerning the foreign trade of agricultural products. By supporting these Northern financial dealings, Watson accused this group of Southern Democrats of "learning [sic] their place in American history by the side of Benedict Arnold." He pleaded with the Macon audience to "cast shame to a people who would surrender principles for the spoils of office."

After denouncing the Northern influence in the Democratic party, Watson turned his metaphorical attack specifically to Henry Grady. The major point of contention that Watson had with Grady was concerning the proper vision of Southern agriculture. Watson asserted that:

> the agriculture situation is gloomy in all parts of the Union. No denying it. Mr. Grady in his great Dallas speech thinks that "plenty rides on the Springing harvests!" It rides on Grady's springing imagination. Where is this prosperity?[53]

---

[53]Watson Papers, *Journal #2*, 419.

Watson directly contradicted Grady's perceptions of the real economic condition facing the rural Georgia farmer. The visionary metaphors presented by Grady were simply unrealistic in Watson's assessment of poor farmers in the South. Concerning this error in vision, Watson argued: "It's like these city fellows to draw ideal pictures of farm life—pictures which are no more true to life than a fashion plate is to an actual man or woman—or a photograph is to the original."[54]

In contrast to the unrealistic "transfiguration of farm life" in the South presented by Grady, Watson suggested that the "big city editor" was tragically ignoring the very real problems outside the urban confines of Atlanta. For example, Watson told his audience:

> In Grady's farm life there are no poor cows. They are all fat! Their bells twinkle musically in clover scented meadows and all you have to do is hold a pan under the udder and catch it full of golden Jersey butter.[55]

Watson presented his view of Southern farm life in very different metaphors than those of Grady:

> In real life, we find the poor bridled cow—with wolves on her back, "hollow horn" on her head, and she always wants to back up where the wind wouldn't play a tune on her ribs and when you milk her, you get the genuine "blue milk"—which being laboriously churned out till profanity would be a blessed relief produces a butter of more different colors than Joseph's coat and more different tastes than you find between the shells of a wild turtle.[56]

Beyond the many errors displayed in the Grady speeches about Southern agriculture, Watson wanted his listeners to see how much of a traitor the editor was concerning the South's future. Grady's address in Dallas was, in Watson's view, evidence of regional treachery:

> Grady's speech is an indictment against us. He only comments on our sins! Nothing is said of those who sin against us . . . But what of the trespasses against us? Banking laws—Brazil helping her farmers with

---

[54]Watson Papers, *Journal* #2, 419.
[55]Watson Papers, *Journal* #2, 419.
[56]Watson Papers, *Journal* #2, 420.

$6,000,000 loan—in contrast to here. We are denied access to currency
which is the life blood of enterprise.[57]

Besides the banking laws, Watson also argued that Grady neglected to
mention how the 81.5 percent tariff rates actually helped to cause the
problems faced by Southern farmers. While Watson agreed that diver-
sifying crops might help the situation, he cautioned that this would "not
cure the many evils allied against the farmer." Instead of following
Grady's plan calling for Southern financial and industrial dependence on
the North, Watson urged: "[L]et us of the South move closer together and
comfort ourselves with the sympathy of our common interests —our great
family held together by mutual affection and sorrow and purpose."[58]

Watson concluded the Macon Fair speech by reminding his audience
that while "speakers die, their words of truth" never do. Someday in the
future, Watson noted, his words of truth would "flow down the streams
of thought" and eventually "find congenial soil in the hearts and minds
of the people of the South."

Tom Watson failed in his bid to be chosen as presidential elector at
large for the state of Georgia in 1888. By the end of the decade, Watson
had abandoned the Democratic Party and turned his reform efforts full
time to the radical politics of the Southern Farmer's Alliance and its
"People's Party." These organizations attempted to unify Southern and
Midwestern farmers into a solid voting block between 1892 and 1896.
Ultimately, these political efforts failed, but Watson's rhetoric maintained
its strong metaphorical vision of the proper role of poor farmers, white
and black, throughout the decade of the 1890s.[59] These later political developments had their rhetorical origins in the verbal struggle that Watson
engaged in with Henry Grady during the late 1880s.[60]

---

[57]Watson Papers, *Journal #2*, 421.

[58]Watson Papers, *Journal #2*, 422.

[59]The texts of some of Watson's speeches during this period are available in
Norman Pollack, ed. *The Populist Mind* (Indianapolis: The Bobbs-Merrill Company,
1967).

[60]See, for example, C. Vann Woodward, *Tom Watson*, 113-28.

Watson's Metaphors: The Vision Unified

Beginning with his early ceremonial speeches in 1880, Tom Watson's metaphors provided a vision of how the poor Southerner should think about and conduct business in the future. Watson drew heavily upon his own personal experiences with agriculture and his close understanding of the cruelties of rural life. The metaphors Watson used early in the decade revealed his thinking about the dark, stormy, and unpredictable existence that Georgia farmers had to endure.

Watson's Penfield and Greensboro speeches expressed an evolving metaphoric vision of optimism for the farmer if specific warnings were respected by the young. He believed that Georgia farmers could succeed, but only if they held to their sense of independence and became self-sufficient again as they had before the war. Watson recognized that the Old South traditions would never return; however, the dependency on agriculture would remain for decades to come. In the early speeches of the 1880s, "independence" emerged as a key metaphor indicating Watson's belief that the lessons taught by Southern pride and honor were still true. Watson assured his rural listeners that delays in agricultural progress were due to the outside influence of greedy Northern bankers and merchants.

Toward the middle of the decade, Watson's speeches began to contain metaphors that suggested his growing concern with the changing attitudes about commerce and agriculture. Since the traditional way of conducting business was under attack throughout the South, Watson's metaphors offered a return to the comfort and security of the old ways of thinking about personal labor and its intrinsic value to society. Watson's commencement address at Mercer University warned against any alterations in the way Southerners typically thought about work. By becoming too skeptical and believing that hard personal effort meant nothing since positions could be "purchased at a price," Watson argued that this new creed of materialism paled by comparison to the pride and honor of the Old South. Through dark metaphors, Watson held up oral examples of the new creed for his rural audiences and demanded an overall comparison to the "truth" as embodied in the traditions of the Old South. With Robert E. Lee as the symbolic embodiment of all "true" Southern virtues, Watson's illustrations were particularly vivid in describing the positive values of antebellum Southern life.

Watson's final speeches in 1888 completed a metaphorical evolution into a defensive vision designed to maintain unity among poor Southern farmers. With the battlelines in the new economic order drawn against farmers, Watson asserted that the agrarian way of life still offered the correct path to cultural harmony and spiritual truth for the South. The growth of a competition mentality with farmers and merchants devouring each other for mere financial gain hastened the decline of morality and Southern honor. Watson pleaded for poor Southern farmers to recognize their common distress and join together in a unified political struggle against those supporting the rise of personally destructive economic systems.

Once Watson identified Grady as the key spokesman for the new industrial order, he attempted to force audiences into a comparison of the different visions between the "old" and "new" South. Watson organized his speeches in such a way as to allow listeners to conceptualize the errors and inconsistencies in Grady's vision. The logical result of Watson's comparisons was the conclusion that Grady's thinking about Southern agriculture was destructive and unrealistic. Since Grady lacked any personal understanding of the farmer's problems, how could he recommend a financial union with Northern bankers or merchants that would actually benefit Southern agriculture?

For Watson, the "Solid South" metaphor came to embody that traditional mode of thinking about Southern self-sufficiency and independence. Watson also used this metaphor to demonstrate his goals of keeping the Southern branch of the Democratic Party unified against Northern interference. Just as the South came together as a unified region to fight a war to defend its traditions and sense of honor, Watson's metaphors defended the Cavalier creed and resisted any transition in thinking that might threaten this ideology. Watson's defensive vision was not necessarily anti-progressive, but it did maintain an honorable place for the poor Southern farmer. Since Grady's new industrial creed neglected to include a realistic identity for farmers, white or black, Watson's metaphors helped to fill in the mental gaps and provide a vocabulary for how these traditional Southern agrarians could talk about their future.

Chapter 4

Through the Matrix of Metaphors

"The traditional southern mode of discourses presupposes someone at the other end silently listening; it is the rhetorical mode."

—Allen Tate
Studies in American Culture

"Any important reform, any revolution demands a renewal of vocabulary. Men have not been transformed so long as their way of thinking has remained unchanged."

—Georges Gusdorf
La Parole

In the words of Richard Weaver, Henry Grady and Tom Watson did their rhetorical best in the 1880s to advise Southerners by publicly "showing them better versions of themselves."[1] With the evidence of Civil War destruction all around the South, Grady and Watson offered direction and hope for an uncharted future. As the preceding chapters demonstrate, the rhetorical tool they most often used was a futuristic vision laden with powerful metaphors that helped to bridge the lost past with a newly found future.

This chapter will detail the symbolic power of these metaphors as interpretations of the past and will consider the associated potency of Grady's and Watson's metaphors for symbolically linking the past to their visions of the future. Finally, the chapter will treat their rhetorical inventions as crucial instruments of personal and regional identification during the late 1880s.

---

[1]Richard Weaver, *The Ethics of Rhetoric* (South Bend, Indiana: Gateway Editions, 1953) 25.

Setting the Stage:
Metaphors and Remembrance of Things Past

Before Watson and Grady could articulate a vision for the South's future, they first had to restructure the Southern past. Grady, in his New South speech, was particularly effective in demonstrating how similar were Northerners and Southerners. At the outset of this speech, Grady outlined the early differences between Puritan and Cavalier and then transformed these past figures into a post-Revolutionary "American citizen." In this rhetorical transfiguration, the regional animosities that led up to the Civil War were quickly set aside or denied. Finally, he offered his listeners a model, if unlikely citizen—Abraham Lincoln. While Henry Grady did not actually apologize for the South and the Civil War, his futuristic metaphors helped to lay aside the issue of who caused the conflict and indicated that both regions were of similar mind and now could revere the memory of a martyred president. Absent from the Grady vision was any hint that Lincoln's election was the political spark that eventually led to the Civil War.

Asserting that the South had for too long "rested everything on slavery and agriculture," Grady described the weary ex-Confederate soldier returning to his old homestead moneyless, creditless, and without the training or experience for the future. Even without any "payment for four years of sacrifice," these veterans, in the Grady vision, returned to farming and quickly had lush green harvests by June. But Grady observed that despite the good harvests the Southerner was now ready to accept the fact that agriculture "could neither give nor maintain healthy economic growth."

Grady's use of new metaphors to attribute economic motives for the Civil War established the need for a different future for the South. Southerners did work hard after returning to their farms, but Grady's transfiguration presented a new actuality of experience for his listeners. As Aristotle has noted, lively metaphors place unlikely and surprising pictures of similarity before an audience and therefore create a deception.[2] This new economic incentive for the war was far from the high moral

---

[2]Lane Cooper, trans., *The Rhetoric of Aristotle* (Englewood Cliffs, New Jersey: Prentice Hall, 1932) 212-13.

principles argued by such Southern leaders as John C. Calhoun and Robert Toombs.

In Grady's Dallas speech, he completed a rhetorical transformation of the South's past. Grady argued that the soldier-farmer was committed to the progress of the Union. The only problem standing in the way of this new unity was how to deal with the ex-slave in the Southern economy. Grady reassured his listeners that the Negro's lowly status would remain unchanged in the new economic order, and white Southerners readily accepted his references to the Great Chain of Being social hierarchy. The editor recommended that white Southern soldiers leave the fields and find their fortunes in the towns and cities of the South, but he failed to mention that many ex-slaves had left the farms during Reconstruction to find their fortunes there as well.[3]

The rhetoric of Tom Watson echoed in stark contrast to the vision of the South's past presented by Grady. Watson's speeches depicted the Southern farmer as one who relished the independence and hard work involved with plowing the land. Watson populated the post-Civil War South with "lords of the soil" rather than farmers—they would endure great hardships and might have to wait until the afterlife for the Lord's banquet. He believed Southern farmers had the potential for prosperity, but this must come slowly if they stood with their traditions of Southern honor and personal independence.

Watson's early speeches maintained a tone of discomfort, even bitterness toward changes in tradition. Rather than Grady's Lincoln model of national unity, Watson offered Robert E. Lee, Alexander Stephens and Robert Toombs. He encouraged Southerners to channel their past warrior spirit into conquering the stormy economic problems of the present. While the Cavalier spirit of honor and forbearance was still very much alive in the rural South, Watson ignored the instances of cruelty to slaves that helped to support the old creed of Southern gentility. He linked the heroism and virtue of Lee, Toombs, and Stephens with the slavery-supported Old South agriculture kingdom. He pleaded with his audiences for the preservation of honor and pride in the memory of the Old South. Watson's version of this Southern past used metaphors that ignored the ugly scars of slavery.

---

[3]See C. Vann Woodward. *Origins of the New South: 1877-1913* (Baton Rouge: Louisiana State University Press, 1951) 207-209.

The final transfiguration of the South's past that emerged from Watson's metaphors in the late 1880s were references to political unity. By describing the forces of the North in political or military battle with a Solid South, Watson recalled the Southern Jeffersonian-Jacksonian tradition of standing in unity with fellow farmers. These great presidents had waged a powerful struggle against the disciples of Alexander Hamilton, who sought to forge an elitist society dominated by the wealthy classes. The coming battles against the new centralists or materialists, Watson observed, would have to be fought along the same lines of moral principle that Southerners had engaged in before. Since the poor Southern farmer still maintained his time-honored place as proud lord of the soil, Watson concluded that political and social solidarity molded like those of past conquests would eventually bring victory.

A New Truth Revealed: Metaphors and the Future

After Grady and Watson had transformed the South's past, these rhetors moved next to present the future. Grady and Watson assumed that they addressed an audience of the entire South; however, their messages were suitable only to select groups throughout the region. Trained for Southern leadership, Grady spoke for the Southern middle class and to the Northern industrial elite. Except for his Elberton speech, most of Grady's rhetoric was directed to a Northern audience; he sought financial support for Atlanta and the major cities of the South. By contrast, Watson delivered his major speeches in Georgia to mostly rural audiences.

Grady offered his Northern and Southern audience the brightest, most positive metaphors possible. Instead of the isolated Georgia dirt farmer merely growing a few crops for subsistence and a little pocket money on the side, Grady wanted the soldier-farmer to dedicate himself to a new revolution in agriculture. Without depending on the old ways of thinking or acting on the planting of single crops like cotton, the farmer of Grady's New South was to see himself as a merchant to the world selling a widely diversified variety of crops as produce to consumers. Grady said the Southern soil had the potential to supply far more than just cotton. In partnership of science, the new Southern merchant of the world could locate and dominate an ever-expanding market for his goods.

Grady recognized that there would be some opposition to the transformation of Southern agriculture. The major problem, the existence of poor ex-slaves around the Southern countryside, would take care of itself if the ambitious white farmer would simply leave his land and find his fortune in the industrial meccas of cities and towns. (While Grady did encourage Southerners to leave the farm life, his Elberton speech specifically praised rural living and warned against moving to the city. The New South vision for Grady was complex and often contradictory as he struggled to maintain political unity.) Since blacks were mentally inferior, they would remain on the land to help supply food to the fast-growing Southern city. Above all, Grady warned, the white Southerner must stand with his brothers in political battle and demonstrate to the North that the Republicans could not hope to find a political foothold in the South. Southern whites were to forget their class distinctions and vote to retain the traditional Democratic leadership in the region. By minimizing political, class, and race problems in the South, Grady hoped to influence Northern investors that the South's future was a calm environment in which to invest their money and to develop industry.

Grady's metaphors reveal that he feared political division, or at least the perception of societal conflict for Northern financial leaders. He did not, however, fear the consequences of the scramble for world markets envisioned in his geographical "chessboard." With the benefit of enough capital and educational support from the North, all white residents of the South, rich and poor, urban and rural, would eventually share in a very economically-secure future. In his University of Virginia and Elberton speeches, Grady pleaded with the poor Southern farmer to stay with the Democratic Party and resist the temptation to form a third party. Using the threat of industrial monopolies and centralized wealth of the Republicans as penalties for deserting the Democrats, Grady ultimately asked the farmers throughout the South to have patience until the existing political system defeated the Republicans. Once the Democrats were firmly in power, Grady envisioned that the poor farmer would soon be the recipient of the first benefits from education and science.

Since Henry Grady died long before he could see most of his futuristic vision for the South come true, it would be impossible to predict how the editor might have altered his rhetoric in the 1890s. His lack of sensitivity for poor black and white farmers, however, has been harshly criticized by some historians.[4] In one of the harshest critiques of the Grady vision, the rhetorical scholar Harold Mixon claims that not only were the editor's claims overly extravagant, but that there was a very wide "gap between his claims and reality."[5] In his final appraisal, Mixon argues that Grady's rhetoric succeeded "primarily because his strategy rationalized for his audiences what they *wanted* to hold." This was certainly true, but it must also be noted that the emotionally-charged metaphors that Grady urged upon his white middle-class audience provided a successful comparison between the unreachable past and a most promising economic future. Grady's vision of the future was not the only one competing for public acceptance in the South, but his unique New South metaphor was the vision that eventually received the most attention both inside and outside the region.

Watson's vision for the South's future contained metaphors of tension and conflict. Even as a young lawyer, Watson lashed out at the subtle changes that he detected in the Southern way of life during the 1880s. In his early ceremonial speeches, Watson also offered a vision of hope for the suffering farmer. Since Watson had himself been reared on an impoverished farm, he was well aware of the spiritual needs of the tenant family. These rural audiences that Watson addressed, however, needed a sense of hope and direction that was missing in Grady's rhetoric. While both Watson and Grady could talk about the need for capital throughout the South, it was only Watson that demonstrated a sensitivity to the specific economic needs of the Georgia dirt farmer.

From the beginning of the 1880s, Watson warned against the dangers of outside entanglements with the financial lords in the industrial North. Watson's aspirations for the South called for a careful maintenance of the traditional honor, pride, and personal independence that had long marked the cultural uniqueness of Southerners. Watson could not see how anyone in the South could ethically do business with industrialists of the North who erected stiff tariff barriers—barriers that lowered the eventual profit that farmers received for their crops when shipped to foreign markets. Inconsistencies such as these were part of the rhetorical arsenal that Watson used against Grady's New South sentiments.

---

[4]See, for example, Numan V. Bartley, *The Creation of Modern Georgia* (Athens: University of Georgia Press, 1983) 83-86.

[5]Harold D. Mixon, "Henry Grady as a Persuasive Strategist," in *Oratory in the New South*, ed. Braden, 109-11.

In his Mercer and Milledgeville speeches, Watson spoke specifically against the underlying philosophy behind the New South Creed. Attacking the new creed as cultural skepticism, Watson asserted that the lust for money and material gain tended to cheapen the quality of life and allow Southern society to drift too far from its traditional values and cultural truths. If all things assumed a price, then trust and personal loyalty, in the Watson vision, would foment the rise of a crushing economic competition. In both the Mercer and Milledgeville speeches, Watson used the "big fish" devouring the "small fish" metaphor to demonstrate the eventual result of personal competition in a market-dominated economy. Even with the declining charm of farming, he tried to explain to the Milledgeville graduates that—compared with the harsh world of industry—agriculture could be saved if Southerners would realize that this traditional way of life was being threatened.

To save Southern agriculture, Watson eventually helped create a third party—a true People's Party. During the late 1880s, however, Watson worked to reform the Democratic Party against the proposals so often supported by Grady that so often hurt farmers. Watson feared the Republicans as did Grady, but he refused to support Grover Cleveland unless the Democratic position on such things as the tariff was greatly modified. After observing the insensitivity of Grady to the poor farmer's plight, Watson directly attacked the editor in three speeches during 1888. In these speeches, Watson told his rural audience that Grady's metaphors specifically excluded them and ignored economic reality. Instead of a racially-divided New South, Watson advocated a political Solid South of poor white and black farmers.

Most scholarly accounts of Watson's vision of reform conclude with the sentiment that in spite of the Georgian's courage and fighting spirit, he "struggled but failed."[6] And while some rhetoricians like Jack Gravlee label Watson a "demagogue," the same author also admits that the early career of the orator was one of humane justice and that many of the Populist ideas he advocated in the 1880s were later endorsed by the major parties and became law.[7] A portion of the rhetorical success enjoyed by

---

[6]C. Vann Woodward, *Tom Watson: Agrarian Rebel* (London: Oxford University Press, 1938) 486; See also C. Vann Woodward, *Thinking Back: The Perils of Writing History* (Baton Rouge: Louisiana State University Press, 1986) Chapter 2.

[7]G. Jack Gravlee, "Tom Watson: Disciple of Jeffersonian Democracy," in *The Oratory of Southern Demagogues,* ed. Louge and Dorgan, 106-107.

Watson during this era should be attributed to his ability to exploit the gap apparent in the Grady metaphor concerning the Southern farmer. The aggressive metaphors used by Watson to express his vision of the South's future reached disenchanted farmers throughout the region, and Watson's rhetoric was that most often heeded by rebellious agrarians in the late 1880s and early 1890s.

Metaphors and Southern Identity

The visions of the South's future metaphorically presented to Southerners of the 1880s by Grady and Watson offered much more than a choice of direction for poor farmers and middle-class merchants. Inherent in their rhetoric was a unique vocabulary of metaphors that facilitated the transition of Southern thought from military Reconstruction to economic security. The new metaphors depicted important similarities or mental associations with the key symbols of the South's past. They were designed to transform the thinking of Southerners about their new future.[8]

With the decline of Southern agriculture in the 1880s and the rise of industrialization, a revolution was taking place in the everyday life and experiences of the Southerner. As Georges Gusdorf has observed, "[A]ny revolution demands a renewal of vocabulary; men have not been transformed so long as their way of speaking has remained unchanged."[9] The rhetorical power of Watson's and Grady's metaphors forced attentive Southerners to choose among these visions for talking about the different futures that were competing for their acceptance. By using the Watson or Grady vocabulary in their everyday dialogue to explain and comprehend the future, the real rhetorical significance of metaphors to the Southern mind became evident.

The pervasiveness of the Grady metaphors after 1889 has been well documented by Paul Gaston. Even though the small ruling class of Southern merchants, industrialists, and wealthy planters benefited from Grady's New South Creed, Gaston argues that the new vocabulary helped to forge a cultural ideology of a "powerful social myth, further strengthening the

---

[8]Colin M. Turbayne, *The Myth of Metaphor* (New Haven: Yale University Press, 1962) 57.

[9]Georges Gusdorf, *Speaking La Parole* (Evanston: Northwestern University Press, 1965) 15.

existing order and impressing upon Southerners a pattern of belief that would be increasingly difficult to throw off."[10] While Gaston may well explain the spread of Grady's new ideology, the transformative power of metaphor in rhetoric helps better display the "special mental and material forces that have shaped the southern experience."[11] The occurrence today of Grady's New South vocabulary in modern ceremonial and political speeches may lack the detailed vision that the editor rhetorically created in the 1880s, but their reappearance indicate that these original metaphors still work in Southern dialogue.[12]

The social impact of Tom Watson's metaphors can be demonstrated in his rhetorical influence on the Populist movement of the 1890s. By 1896, poor rebellious farmers in the South and West came together in the largest mass movement in American history.[13] Lawrence Goodwyn has argued that Watson contributed to this movement a "spirit of collective hope for a better future." Watson's rhetoric also helped to animate American Populism by offering "vibrant moments of shared effort that provided the evidence of its vitality, its aspirations, and its defeats."[14] Through his aggressive metaphors like those used against Grady's New South Creed, Watson tried to bring poor Southern farmers together in the 1880s by showing them that the Grady vision had no real meaning for them. In his speeches of 1888, Watson graphically explained how alien the Grady vocabulary was for describing the harsh life on the Southern farm.[15] As economic conditions worsen for farmers of the 1990s,

---

[10]Paul M. Gaston, *The New South Creed: A Study in Southern Mythmaking* (Baton Rouge: Louisiana State University Press, 1976) 219-20.

[11]Gaston, 245.

[12]See, for example, John D. Saxon, "Contemporary Southern Oratory: A Rhetoric of Hope Not Desperation," *Southern Speech Communication Journal* 40 (Spring 1975) 262-74; and Jerry Himelstein, "Rhetorical Continuities in the Politics of Race: The Closed Society Revisited," *Southern Speech Communication Journal* 48 (Winter 1983) 153-66. See also Stephen A. Smith, *Myth, Media and the Southern Mind*, (Fayetteville: University of Arkansas Press, 1985) 1-4.

[13]Lawrence Goodwyn, *The Populist Moment* (London: Oxford University Press, 1978) vii.

[14]Goodwyn, 277.

[15]Tom Watson later published a "handbook" for "Editors, Speakers, and Lecturers" explaining in detail the meaning of most of the Populist vocabulary. See the modern reprint of this 1892 work in Thomas E. Watson, *The People's Party Campaign Book, 1892* (New York: Arno Press, 1975).

Watson's metaphors pleading with farmers to "stand together" echoes in the cultural dialogue of our time.[16]

Since the rhetorical influence of Watson's and Grady's struggle of the 1880s is still prevalent in the Southern vocabulary, it would be difficult to trace the transformation in metaphors from 1888 to the present. It is evident, however, that the two visions oratorically presented in the 1880s by Grady and Watson signalled an important transition in Southern dialogue. By focusing on the metaphors that formed the genesis of that rhetorical transformation, this study has offered a demonstration of how the speeches of Grady and Watson shaped the Southern experience.

---

[16]See, for example, C. Vann Woodward, "The Ghost of Populism Walks Again," *The New York Times Magazine*, 4 June 1972, 16-69; Lawrence Goodwyn, "The New Populism: A Hell-Raising Tradition Waits to be Reborn," *The Progressive* 48 (June 1984): 18-20; and Bill Lambrecht, "Talk of Loans Lures Farmers to Extremist Groups," *St. Louis Post-Dispatch*, 20 May 1984, 1.

Appendix A

Key Speeches of Henry Grady

Grady's New South Speech

[Henry W. Grady's "New South Speech," presented to the New England Society, New York City, 21 December 1886. The text is from the *Atlanta Constitution*, 22 December 1886.]

"There was a South of slavery and secession—that South is dead. There is a South of union and freedom—that South, thank God, is living, breathing, growing every hour." These words, delivered from the immortal lips of Benjamin H. Hill, at Tammany Hall, in 1866, true then and truer now, I shall make my text to-night.

Mr. President and Gentlemen: Let me express to you my appreciation of the kindness by which I am permitted to address you. I make this abrupt acknowledgment advisedly, for I feel that if, when I raise my provincial voice in this ancient and august presence, I could find courage for no more than the opening sentence, it would be well if in that sentence I had met in a rough sense my obligation as a guest, and had perished, so to speak, with courtesy on my lips and grace in my heart. Permitted, through your kindness, to catch my second wind, let me say that I appreciate the significance of being the first Southerner to speak at this board, which bears the substance, if it surpasses the semblance, of original New England hospitality—and honors the sentiment that in turn honors you, but in which my personality is lost, and the compliment to my people made plain.

I bespeak the utmost stretch of your courtesy to-night. I am not troubled about those from whom I come. You remember the man whose wife sent him to a neighbor with a pitcher of milk, and who, tripping on the top step, fell with such casual interruptions as the landings afforded into the basement, and, while picking himself up, had the pleasure of hearing his wife call out: "John did you break the pitcher?"

"No, I didn't," said John, "but I'll be dinged if I don't."

So, while those who call me from behind may inspire me with energy, if not with courage, I ask an indulgent hearing from you. I beg that you will bring your full faith in American fairness and frankness to judgment upon what I shall say. There was an old preacher once who told some boys of the Bible lesson he was going to read in the morning. The boys, finding the place, glued together the connecting pages. The next morning he read on the bottom of one page, "When Noah was one hundred and twenty years old he took unto himself a wife, who was" —then turning the page—"140 cubits. long—40 cubits wide, built of gopher wood—and covered with pitch inside and out." He was naturally puzzled at this. He read it again, verified it, and then said: "My friends, this is the first time I ever met this in the Bible, but I accept this as an evidence of the assertion that we are fearfully and wonderfully made." If I could get you to hold such faith to-night I could proceed cheerfully to the task I otherwise approach with a sense of consecration.

Pardon me one word, Mr. President, spoken for the sole purpose of getting into the volumes that go out annually freighted with the rich eloquence of your speakers—the fact that the Cavalier as well as the Puritan was on the continent in its early days, and that he was "up and able to be about." I have read your books carefully and I find no mention of that fact, which seems to me an important one for preserving a sort of historical equilibrium if for nothing else.

Let me remind you that the Virginia Cavalier first challenged France on the continent—that Cavalier, John Smith, gave New England its very name, and was so pleased with the job that he has been handing his own name around ever since—and that while Miles Standish was cutting off men's ears for courting a girl without her parents' consent, and forbade men to kiss their wives on Sunday, the Cavalier was courting everything in sight, and that the Almighty had vouchsafed great increase to the Cavalier colonies, the huts in the wilderness being as full as the nests in the woods.

But having incorporated the Cavalier as a fact in your charming little books, I shall let him work out his own salvation, as he has always done, with engaging gallantry, and we will hold no controversy as to his merits. Why should we? Neither Puritan nor Cavalier long survived as such. The virtues and good traditions of both happily still live for the inspiration of their sons and the saving of the old fashion. But both Puritan and Cavalier were lost in the storm of the first Revolution, and the American citizen, supplanting both and stronger than either, took possession of the republic bought by their common blood and fashioned to wisdom, and charged himself with teaching men government and establishing the voice of the people as the voice of God.

My friends, Dr. Talmage has told you that the typical American has yet to come. Let me tell you that he has already come. Great types, like valuable plants, are slow to flower and fruit. But from the union of these colonists, Puritans and Cavaliers, from the straightening of their purposes and the crossing of their blood, slow perfecting through a century, came he who stands as the first typical American, the first who comprehended within himself all the strength and gentleness, all the majesty and grace of this republic—Abraham Lincoln. He was the sum of Puritan and Cavalier, for in his ardent nature were fused the virtues of both, and in the depths of his great soul the faults of both were lost. He was greater than Puritan, greater than Cavalier, in that he was American, and that in his honest form were first gathered the vast and thrilling forces of his ideal government—charging it with such tremendous meaning and elevating it above human suffering that martyrdom, though infamously aimed, came as a fitting crown to a life consecrated from the cradle to human liberty. Let us, each cherishing the traditions and honoring his fathers, build with reverent hands to the type of this simple but sublime life, in which all types are honored, and in our common glory as Americans there will be plenty and to spare for your forefathers and for mine.

Dr. Talmage has drawn for you, with a master's hand, the picture of your returning armies. He has told you how, in the pomp and circumstance of war, they came back to you, marching with proud and victorious tread, reading their glory in a nation's eye! Will you bear with me while I tell you of another army that sought its home at the close of the late war—an army that marched home in defeat and not in victory—in pathos and not in splendor, but in glory that equaled yours, and to hearts as loving as ever welcomed heroes home! Let me picture to you the footsore Confederate soldier, as buttoning up in his faded gray jacket the parole which was to bear testimony to his children of his fidelity and faith, he turned his face southward from Appomattox in April, 1865. Think of him as ragged, half-starved, heavy-hearted, enfeebled by wants and wounds, having fought to exhaustion, he surrenders his gun, wrings the hands of his comrades in silence, and lifting his tear-stained and pallid face for the last time to the graves that dot old Virginia hills, pulls his gray cap over his brow and begins the slow and painful journey. What does he find—let me ask you who went to your homes eager to find, in the welcome you had justly earned, full payment for four years' sacrifice—what does he find when, having followed the battle-stained cross against overwhelming odds, dreading death not half so much as surrender, he reaches the home he left so prosperous and beautiful? He finds his house in ruins, his farm devastated, his slaves free, his stock killed, his barns empty, his trade destroyed, his money worthless, his social system, feudal in its magnificence, swept away; his people without law or legal status; his comrades slain, and the burdens of others heavy on his shoulders. Crushed by defeat, his very traditions are gone. Without money, credit, employment, material, or training; and beside all this, confronted with the gravest problem that ever met human intelligence —the establishing of a status for the vast body of his liberated slaves.

What does he do—this hero in gray with a heart of gold? Does he sit down in sullenness and despair? Not for a day. Surely God, who has stripped him of his prosperity, inspired him in his adversity. As ruin was never before so overwhelming, never was restoration swifter. The soldier stepped from the trenches into the furrow; horses that had charged Federal guns marched before the plow, and fields that ran red with human blood in April were green with the harvest in June; women reared in luxury cut up their dresses and made breeches for their husbands, and, with a patience and heroism that fit women always as a garment, gave their hands to work. There was little bitterness in all this. Cheerfulness and frankness prevailed. "Bill Arp" struck the key-note when he said: "Well, I killed as many of them as they did of me, and now I'm going to work." Of the soldier returning home after defeat and roasting some corn on the roadside, who made the remark to his comrades: "You may leave the South if you want to, but I am going to Sandersville, kiss my wife and raise a crop, and if the Yankees fool with me any more, I'll whip 'em again." I want to say to General Sherman, who is considered an able man in our parts, though some people think he is a kind of careless man about fire, that from the ashes he left us in 1864 we have raised a brave and beautiful city; that somehow or other we have caught the sunshine in the bricks and mortar of our homes, and have builded therein not one ignoble prejudice or memory.

But what is the sum of our work? We have found out that in the summing up the free negro counts more than he did as a slave. We have planted the schoolhouse on the hilltop and made it free to white and black. We have sowed towns and cities in the place of theories, and put business above politics. We have challenged your spinners in Massachusetts and your iron-makers in Pennsylvania. We have learned that the $400,000,000 annually received from our cotton crop will make us rich when the supplies that make it are home-raised. We have reduced the commercial rate of interest from 24 to 6 per cent., and are floating 4 per cent. bonds. We have learned that one northern immigrant is worth fifty foreigners; and have smoothed the path to southward, wiped out the place where Mason and Dixon's line used to be, and hung out latchstring to you and yours. We have reached the point that marks perfect harmony in every household, when the husband confesses that the pies which his wife cooks are as good as those his mother used to bake; and we admit that the sun shines as brightly and the moon as softly as it did before the war. We have established thrift in city and country. We have fallen in love with work. We have restored comfort to homes from which culture and elegance never departed. We have let economy take root and spread among us as rank as the crabgrass which sprung from Sherman's cavalry camps, until we are ready to lay odds on the Georgia Yankee as he manufactures relics of the battlefield in a one-story shanty and squeezes pure olive oil out of his cotton seed, against any down-easter that ever swapped wooden nutmegs for flannel sausage in the valleys of Vermont. Above all, we know that we have achieved in these "piping times of peace" a fuller independence for the South than that which our fathers sought to win in the forum by their eloquence or compel in the field by their swords.

It is a rare privilege, sir, to have had part, however humble, in this work. Never was nobler duty confided to human hands than the uplifting and upbuilding of the prostrate and bleeding South—misguided, perhaps, but beautiful in her suffering, and honest, brave and generous always. In the record of her social, industrial and political illustration we await with confidence the verdict of the world.

But what of the negro? Have we solved the problem he presents or progressed in honor and equity toward solution? Let the record speak to the point. No section shows a more prosperous laboring population than the negroes of the South, none in fuller sympathy with the employing and land-owning class. He shares our school fund, has the fullest protection of our laws and the friendship of our people. Self-interest, as well as honor, demand that he should have this. Our future, our very existence depend upon our working out this problem in full and exact justice. We understand that when Lincoln signed the emancipation proclamation, your victory was assured, for he then committed you to the cause of human liberty, against which the arms of man cannot prevail—while those of our statesmen who trusted to make slavery the corner-stone of the Confederacy doomed us to defeat as far as they could, committing us to a cause that reason could not defend or the sword maintain in sight of advancing civilization.

Had Mr. Toombs said, which he did not say, "that he would call the roll of his slaves at the foot of Bunker Hill," he would have been foolish, for he might have known that whenever slavery became entangled in war it must perish, and that the chattel in human flesh ended forever in New England when your fathers—not to be blamed for parting with what didn't pay—sold their slaves to our fathers—not to be praised for knowing a paying thing when they saw it. The relations of the southern people with the negro are close and cordial. We remember with what fidelity for four years he guarded our defenseless women and children, whose husbands and fathers were fighting against his freedom. To his eternal credit be it said that whenever he struck a blow for his own liberty he fought in open battle, and when at last he raised his black and humble hands that the shackles might be stuck off, those hands were innocent of wrong against his helpless charges, and worthy to be taken in loving grasp by every man who honors loyalty and devotion. Ruffians have maltreated him, rascals have misled him, philanthropists established a bank for him, but the South, with the North, protests against injustice to this simple and sincere people. To liberty and enfranchisement is as far as law can carry the negro. The rest must be left to conscience and common sense. It must be left to those among whom his lot is cast, with whom he is indissolubly connected, and whose prosperity depends upon their possessing his intelligent sympathy and confidence. Faith has been kept with him, in spite of calumnious assertions to the contrary by those who assume to speak for us or by frank opponents. Faith will be kept with him in the future, if the South holds her reason and integrity.

But have we kept faith with you? In the fullest sense, yes. When Lee surrendered—I don't say when Johnston surrendered, because I understand he still alludes to the time when he met General Sherman last as the time when he determined to abandon any further prosecution of the struggle—when Lee surrendered, I say, and Johnston quit, the South became, and has since been, loyal to this Union. We fought hard enough to know that we were whipped, and in perfect frankness accept as final the arbitrament of the sword to which we had appealed. The South found her jewel in the toad's head of defeat. The shackles that had held her in narrow limitations fell forever when the shackles of the negro slave were broken. Under the old régime the negroes were slaves to the South; the South was a slave to the system. The old plantation, with the simple police regulations and feudal habit, was the only type possible under slavery. Thus was gathered in the hands of a splendid and chivalric oligarchy the substance that should have been diffused among the people, as the rich blood, under certain artificial conditions, is gathered at the heart, filling that with affluent rapture but leaving the body chill and colorless.

The old South rested everything on slavery and agriculture unconscious that these could neither give nor maintain healthy growth. The new South presents a perfect democracy, the oligarchs leading in the popular movement—a social system compact and closely knitted, less splendid on the surface, but stronger at the core—a hundred farms for every plantation, fifty homes for every palace—and a diversified industry that meets the complex need of this complex age.

The new South is enamored of her new work. Her soul is stirred with the breath of a new life. The light of a grander day is falling fair on her face. She is thrilling with the consciousness of growing power and prosperity. As she stands upright, full-statured and equal among the people of the earth, breathing the keen air and looking out upon the expanded horizon, she understands that her emancipation came because through the inscrutable wisdom of God her honest purpose was crossed, and her brave armies were beaten.

This is said in no spirit of time-serving or apology. The South has nothing for which to apologize. She believes that the late struggle between the States was war and not rebellion; revolution and not conspiracy, and that her convictions were as honest as yours. I should be unjust to the dauntless spirit of the South and to my own convictions if I did not make this plain in this presence. The South has nothing to take back. In my native town of Athens is a monument that crowns its central hill—a plain, white shaft. Deep cut into its shining side is a name dear to me above the names of men—that of a brave and simple man who died in brave and simple faith. Not for all the glories of New England, from Plymouth Rock all the way, would I exchange the heritage he left me in his soldier's death. To the foot of that I shall send my children's children to reverence him who ennobled their name with his heroic blood. But, sir, speaking from the shadow of that memory which I honor as I do nothing else on earth, I say that the cause in which he suffered and for which he gave his life was adjudged by higher and fuller wisdom than his or mine, and I am glad that the omniscient God held the balance of battle in His Almighty hand and that human slavery was swept forever from American soil, the American Union was saved from the wreck of war.

This message, Mr. President, comes to you from consecrated ground. Every foot of soil about the city in which I live is as sacred as a battleground of the republic. Every hill that invests it is hallowed to you by the blood of your brothers who died for your victory, and doubly hallowed to us by the blow of those who died hopeless, but undaunted, in defeat— sacred soil to all of us—rich with memories that make us purer and stronger and better—silent but staunch witnesses in its red desolation of the matchless valor of American hearts and the deathless glory of American arms—speaking an eloquent witness in its white peace and prosperity to the indissoluble union of American States and the imperishable brotherhood of the American people.

Now, what answer has New England to this message? Will she transmit the prejudice of war to remain in the hearts of the conquerors, when it has died in the hearts of the conquered? Will she permit this prejudice to the next generation, that in their hearts which never felt the generous ardor of conflict it may perpetuate itself? Will she withhold, save in strained courtesy, the hand which straight from his soldier's heart Grant offered to Lee at Appomattox? Will she make the vision of a restored and happy people, which gathered above the couch of your dying captain, filling his heart with grace; touching his lips with praise, and glorifying his path to the grave—will she make this vision on which the last sigh of his expiring soul breathed a benediction, a cheat and delusion? If she does, the South, never abject in asking for comradeship, must accept with dignity its refusal; but if she does not refuse to accept in frankness and sincerity this message of good will and friendship, then will the prophecy of Webster, delivered in this very society forty years ago amid tremendous applause, become true, be verified in its fullest sense, when he said: "Standing hand to hand and clasping hands, we should remain united as we have been for sixty years, citizens of the same country, members of the same government, united, all united now and united forever." There have been difficulties, contentions, and controversies, but I tell you that in my judgment,

"Those opened eyes,
Which like the meteors of a troubled heaven,
All of one nature, of one substance bred,
Did lately meet in th' intestine shock,
Shall now, in mutual well beseeming ranks,
March all one way."

Grady's Farmer and the Cities
Speech in Elberton, Georgia

[Henry W. Grady's "The Farmer and the Cities Speech," presented at Elberton, Georgia, 23 July 1889. The text is from the *Atlanta Constitution*, 26 July 1889.]

Mr. President, ladies and gentlemen:—For the first time in my life I address an audience in the open air. And as I stand here in this beautiful morning, so shot through and through with sunshine that the very air is as molten gold to the touch—under these trees in whose trunks the rains and suns of years are compacted, and on whose leaves God has laid His whispering music--here in His majestic temple, with the brightness of His smile breaking all about us—standing above the soil instinct with the touch of His life-giving hand, and full of His promise and His miracle— and looking up to the clouds through which His thunders roll, and His lightnings cut their way, and beyond that to the dazzling glory of the sun, and yet beyond to the unspeakable splendor of the universe, flashing and paling until the separate stars are but as mist in the skies—even to the uplifted jasper gates through which His everlasting glory streams, my mind falls back abashed, and I realize how paltry is human speech, and how idle are the thoughts of men!

Another thought oppresses me. In front of me sit several thousand people. Over there, in smelling distance, where we can almost hear the lisping of the mop as it caresses the barbecued lamb or the pottering of the skewered pig as he leisurely turns from fat to crackling, is being prepared a dinner that I verily believe covers more provisions than were issued to all the soldiers of Lee's army, God bless them, in their last campaign. And I shudder when I think that I, a single, unarmed, defenseless man, is all that stands between this crowd and that dinner. Here then, awed by God's majesty, and menaced by man's appetite, I am tempted to leave this platform and yield to the boyish impulses that always stir in my heart amid such scenes, and revert to the days of boyhood when about the hills of Athens I chased the pacing coon, or twisted the unwary rabbit, or shot my ramrod at all manner of birds and beasts—and at night went home to look up into a pair of gentle eyes and take on my tired face the benediction of a mother's kiss and feel on my weary head a pair of loving hands, now wrinkled and trembling, but, blessed be God, fairer to me yet than the hands of mortal women, and stronger yet to lead me than the hands of mortal man, as they laid a mother's blessing there, while bending at her knees I made my best confession of faith and worshiped at the truest altar I have yet found in this world. I had rather go out and lay down on the ground and hug the grass to my breast and mind me of the time when I builded boyish ambitions on the wooded hills of Athens, than do aught else to-day. But I recall the story of Uncle Remus, who when his favorite hero, Brer Rabbit, was sorely pressed by that arch villain, Brer Fox, said:

"An' Brer Rabbit den he climb'd a tree." "But," said: the little boy, "Uncle Remus, a rabbit can't climb a tree."
"Doan you min' dat, honey. Brer Fox pressed dis rabbit so hard he des bleeged to clim' a tree."

I am pressed so hard to-day by your commands that I am just "bleeged" to make a speech, and so I proceed. I heartily invoke God's guidance in what I say, that I shall utter no word to soil this temple of His, and no sentiment not approved in His wisdom; and as for you, when the time comes—as it will come—when you prefer barbecued shote to raw orator, and feel that you can be happier at that table than in this forum, just say the word and I will be with you heart and soul!

I am tempted to yield to the gaiety of this scene, to the flaunting banners of the trees, the downpouring sunshine, the garnered plenty over there, this smiling and hospitable crowd, and, throwing serious affairs aside, to speak to you to-day as the bird sings—without care and without thought. I should be false to myself and to you if I did, for there are serious problems that beset our State and our country that no man, facing, as I do this morning, a great and intelligent audience, can in honor or in courage disregard. I shall attempt to make no brilliant speech—but to counsel with you in plain and simple words, beseeching your attention and your sympathy as to the dangers of the present hour, and our duties and our responsibilities.

At Saturday noon in any part of this county you may note the farmer going from his field, eating his dinner thoughtfully and then saddling his plow-horse, or starting afoot and making his way to a neighboring church or schoolhouse. There he finds from every farm, through every foot-path, his neighbors gathering to meet him. What is the object of this meeting? It is not social, it is not frolic, it is not a picnic—the earnest thoughtful faces, the serious debate and council, the closed doors and the secret session forbid this assumption. It is a meeting of men who feel that in spite of themselves their affairs are going wrong—of free and equal citizens who feel that they carry unequal burdens—of toilers who feel that they reap not the just fruits of their toil—of men who feel that their labor enriches others while it leases them poor, and that the sweat of their bodies, shed freely under God's command, goes to clothe the idle and the avaricious in purple and fine linen. This is a meeting of protest, o£ resistance. Here the farmer meets to demand, and organize that he may enforce his demand, that he shall stand equal with every other class of citizens—that laws discriminating against him shall be repealed—that the methods oppressing him shall be modified or abolished—and that he shall be guaranteed that neither government nor society shall abridge, by statute or custom, his just and honest proportion of the wealth he created, but that he shall be permitted to garner in his barns, and enjoy by his hearthstone, the full and fair fruits of his labor. If this movement were confined to Elbert, if this disturbing feeling of discontent were shut in the limits of your county lines, it would still demand the attention of the thoughtful and patriotic. But, as it is in Elbert, so it is in every county in Georgia—as in Georgia, so it is in every State in the South—as in the South, so in every agricultural State in the Union. In every rural neighborhood, from Ohio to Texas, from Michigan to Georgia, the farmers, riding thoughtful through field and meadow, seek ten thousand schoolhouses or churches—the muster grounds of this new army—and there, recounting their wrongs and renewing their pledges, send up from neighborhoods to county, from county to State, and State to Republic, the measure of their strength and the unyielding quality of their determination. The agricultural army of the Republic is in motion. The rallying drumbeat has rolled over field and meadow, and from where the wheat locks the sunshine in its bearded sheaf, and the clover carpets the earth, and the cotton whitens beneath the stars, and the tobacco catches the quick aroma of the rains—everywhere that patient man stands above the soil, or bends about the furrow, the farmers are ready in squads and companies and battalions and legions to be led against what they hold to be an oppression that honest men would not deserve, and that brave men would not endure. Let us not fail to comprehend the magnitude and the meaning of this movement. It is no trifling cause that brings the farmers into such determined and widespread organization as this. It is not the skillful arts of the demagogue that has brought nearly two million farmers into this perfect and pledge-bound society—but it is a deep and abiding conviction that, in political and commercial economy of the day, he is put at a disadvantage that keeps him poor while other classes grow rich, and that bars his way to prosperity and independence. General Toombs once said that the farmer, considered the most conservative type of citizenship, is really the most revolutionary. That the farmers of France, flocking to the towns and cities from the unequal burdens of their farms, brought about the French Revolution, and that about once in every century the French peasant raided the towns. Three times the farmers of England have captured and held London. It was the farmers of Mecklenburg that made the first American declaration, and Putnam left his plow standing in the furrow as he hurried to lead the embattled farmers who fought at Concord and Lexington. I realize it is impossible that revolution should be the outcome of our industrial troubles. The farmer of to-day does not consider that remedy for his wrongs. I quote history to show that the farmer, segregated and deliberate, does not move on slight provocation, but organizes only under deep conviction, and that when once organized and convinced, he is terribly in earnest, and is not going to rest until his wrongs are righted.

Now, here we are confronted with the most thorough and widespread agricultural movement of this or any other day. It is the duty alike of farmers and those who stand in other ranks, to get together and consult as to what is the real status and what is the patriotic duty. Not in sullenness, but in frankness. Not as opponents, but as friends—not as enemies, but as brothers begotten of a common mother, banded in common allegiance, and marching to a common destiny. It will not do to say that this organization will pass away, for if the discontent on which it is based survives it, it had better have lived and forced its wrongs to final issue. There is no room for divided hearts in this State, or in this Republic. If we shall restore Georgia to her former greatness and prosperity—if we shall solve the problems that beset the South in honor and safety—if we shall save this Republic from the dangers that threaten it—it will require the earnest and united effort of every patriotic citizen, be he farmer, or merchant, or lawyer, or manufacturer. Let us consider then the situation, and decide what is the duty that lies before us.

In discussing this matter briefly, I beg the ladies to give me their attention. I have always believed that there are few affairs of life in which woman should not have a part. Not obtrusive part—for that is unwomanly. The work falling best to the hand of woman is such work as is done by the dews of night—that ride not on the boasting wind, and shine not in the garish sun, but that come when the wind is stilled and the sun is gone, and night has wrapped the earth in its sacred hush, and fall from the distillery of the stars upon the parched and waiting flowers, as a benediction from God.

Let no one doubt the power of this work, though it lack pomp and circumstance. Is Bismarck the mightiest power of this earth, who is attended by martial strains when he walks abroad, and in whose path thrones are scattered as trophies? Why, the little housewife alone in her chimney-corner, musing in her happiness with no trophy in her path save her husband's loving heart, and no music on her ear save the chirping of the cricket beneath her hearthstone, is his superior. For, while he holds the purse-strings of Germany, she holds the heartstrings of men. She who rocks the cradle rules the world. Give me then your attention, note the conflict that is gathering about us, and take your place with seeming modesty in the ranks of those who fight for right. It is not an abstract political theory that is involved in the contest of which I speak. It is the integrity and independence of your home that is at stake. The battle is not pitched in a distant State. Your home is the battle-field, and by your hearthstones you shall fight for your household gods. With your husband's arms so wound around you that you can feel his anxious heart beating against your cheek—with your sons, sturdy and loving, holding your old hands in theirs—here on the threshold of your house, under the trees that sheltered your babyhood, with the graves of your dead in that plain enclosure yonder—here men and women, heart to heart, with not a man dismayed, not a woman idle—while the multiplied wolves of debt and mortgage, and trust and monopoly, swarm from every thicket; here we must fight the ultimate battle for the independence of our people and the happiness of our homes.

Now let us look at the facts: First, the notable movement of the population in America is from the country to the cities. In 1840—a generation ago, only one-twelfth of the American people lived in cities of more than 8000 people. In 1850, one-eighth; in 1860, one-sixth; in 1870, one-fifth; in 1880, one-fourth. In the past half-century the population of cities has increased more than four times as rapidly as that of the country. Mind you, when I say that the city population has increased in one generation from 8 per cent. to 25 per cent. in population, I mean the population of cities of more than 8000 people. There is not such a city in this congressional district. It is the village and town population, as well as that of the farms, that goes to swell so enormously the population of the great cities. Thus we see diminishing with amazing rapidity that rural population that is the strength and the safety of the people—slow to anger and thus a safeguard, but terrible in its wrath, and thus a tremendous corrective power. No greater calamity could befall any country than the sacrifice of its town and village and country life. I rejoice in Atlanta's growth, and yet I wonder whether it is worth what it cost when I know that her population has been drawn largely from rural Georgia, and that back of her grandeur are thousands of deserted farms and dismantled homes. As much as I love her—and she is all to me that home can be to any man—if I had the disposal of 100,000 immigrants at her gates tomorrow, 5000 should enter there, 75,000 should be located in the shops and factories in Georgia towns and villages, and 20,000 sent to her farms. It saddens me to see a bright young fellow come to my office from village or country, and I shudder when I think for what a feverish and speculative and uncertain life he has bartered his rural birthright, and surrendered the deliberation and tranquillity of his life on the farm. It is just that deliberate life that this country needs, for the fever of the cities is already affecting its system. Character, like corn, is dug from the soil. A contented rural population is not only the measure of our strength, and an assurance of its peace when there should be peace, and a resource of courage when peace would be cowardice—but it is the nursery of the great leaders who have made this country what it is. Washington was born and lived in the country. Jefferson was a farmer. Henry Clay rode his horse to the mill in the slashes. Webster dreamed amid the solitude of Marshfield. Lincoln was a rail splitter. Our own Hill walked between the handles of the plow. Brown peddled barefoot the product of his patch. Stephens found immortality under the trees of his country home. Toombs and Cobb and Calhoun were country gentlemen, and afar from the cities' maddening strife established that greatness that is the heritage of their people. The cities produce very few leaders. Almost every man in our history formed his character in the leisure and deliberation of village or country life, and drew his strength from the drugs of the earth even as a child draws his from his mother's breast. In the diminution of this rural population, virtuous and competent, patriotic and honest, living beneath its own roof-tree, building its altars by its own hearthstone and shrining in its own heart its liberty and its conscience, there is abiding cause for regret. In the corresponding growth of our cities—already center spots of danger, with their idle classes, their sharp rich and poor, their corrupt politics, their consorted thieves, and their clubs and societies of anarchy and socialism—I see a pressing and impending danger. Let it be noted that the professions are crowded, that middlemen are multiplied beyond reason, that the factories can in six months supply the demand of twelve —that machinery is constantly taking the place of men—that labor in every department bids against itself until it is mercilessly in the hands of the employer, that the new-comers are largely recruits of the idle and dangerous classes, and we can appreciate something of the danger that comes with this increasing movement to strip the villages and the farms and send an increasing volume into the already overcrowded cities. This is but one phase of that tendency to centralization and congestion which is threatening the liberties of this people and the life of this Republic.

Now, let us go one step further. What is the most notable financial movement in America? It is the mortgaging of the farm lands of the country—the bringing of the farmer into bondage to the money-lender. In Illinois the farms are mortgaged for $200,000,000, in Iowa for $140,000,000, in Kansas for $160,000,000, and so on through the Northwest. In Georgia about $20,000,000 of foreign capital holds in mortgage perhaps one-fourth of Georgia's farms, and the work is but started. Every town has its loan agent—a dozen companies are quartered in Atlanta, and the work goes briskly on. A mortgage is the bulldog of obligations—a very mud-turtle for holding on. It is the heaviest thing of its weight in the world. I had one once, and sometimes I used to feel, as it rested on my roof, deadening the rain that fell there, and absorbing the sunshine, that it would crush through the shingles and the rafters and overwhelm me with its dull and persistent weight, and when at last I paid it off, I went out to look at the shingles to see if it had not flopped back there of its own accord. Think of it, Iowa strips from her farmers $14,000,000 of interest every year, and sends it to New York and Boston to be reloaned on farms in other States, and to support and establish the dominion of the money-lenders over the people. Georgia gathers from her languishing fields $2,000,000 of interest every year, and sends it away forever. Could her farmers but keep it at home, one year's interest would build factories to supply at cost every yard of bagging and every pound of guano the farmers need, establish her exchanges and their warehouses, and have left more than a million dollars for the improvement of their farms and their homes. And year after year this drain not only continues, but deepens. What will be the end? Ireland has found it. Her peasants in their mud cabins, sending every tithe of their earnings to deepen the purple luxury of London, where their landlords live, realize how poor is that country whose farms are owned in mortgage or fee simple by those who live beyond its borders. If every Irish landlord lived on his estate, bought of his tenants the product of their farms, and invested his rents in Irish industries, this Irish question that is the shame of the world would be settled without legislation or strife. Georgia can never go to Ireland's degradation, but every Georgia farm put under mortgage to a foreign capitalist is a step in that direction, and every dollar sent out as interest leaves the State that much poorer. I do not blame the farmers. It is a miracle that out of their poverty they have done so well. I simply deplore the result, and ask you to note in the millions of acres that annually pass under mortgage to the money-lenders of the East, and in the thousands of independent country homes annually surrendered as hostages to their hands, another evidence of that centralization that is drinking up the life-blood of this broad Republic.

Let us go one step further. All protest as to our industrial condition is met with the statement that America is startling the world with its growth and progress. Is this growth symmetrical—is this progress shared by every class? Let the tax-books of Georgia answer. This year, for the first time since 1860, our taxable wealth is equal to that with which, excluding our slaves, we entered the civil war—$368,000,000. There is cause for rejoicing in this wonderful growth from the ashes and desolation of twenty years ago, but the tax-books show that while the towns and cities are $60,000,000 richer than they were in 1860, the farmers are $50,000,000 poorer.

Who produced this wealth? In 1865, when our towns and cities were paralyzed, when not a mine or quarry was open, hardly a mill or a factory running; when we had neither money or credit, it was the farmers' cotton that started the mills of industry and of trade. Since that desolate year, when, urging his horse down the furrow, plowing through fields on which he had staggered amid the storm of battle, he began the rehabilitation of Georgia with no friend near him save nature that smiled at his kindly touch, and God that sent him the message of cheer through the rustling leaves, he has dug from the soil of Georgia more than $1,000,000,000 worth of product. From this mighty resource great cities have been builded and countless fortunes amassed—but amid all the splendor he has remained the hewer of wood and the drawer of water. He had made the cities $60,000,000 richer than they were when the war began, and he finds himself, in the sweat of whose brow this miracle was wrought, $50,000,000 poorer than he then was. Perhaps not a farmer in this audience knew this fact—but I doubt if there is one in the audience who has not felt in his daily life the disadvantage that in twenty short years has brought about this stupendous difference. Let the figures speak for themselves. The farmer—the first figure to stumble amid the desolate dawn of our new life and to salute the coming day—hurrying to market with the harvest of his hasty planting that Georgia might once more enter the lists of the living States and buy the wherewithal to still her wants and clothe her nakedness—always apparently the master of the situation, has he not been really its slave, when he finds himself at the end of twenty hard and faithful years $110,000,000 out of balance?

Now, let us review the situation a moment. I have shown you, first, that the notable drift of population is to the loss of village and country, and the undue and dangerous growth of the city; second, that the notable movement of finance is that which is bringing villages and country under mortgage to the city; and third, that they who handle the products for sale profit more thereby than those who create them—the difference in one State in twenty years reaching the enormous sum of $110,000,000. Are these healthy tendencies? Do they not demand the earnest and thoughtful consideration of every patriotic citizen? The problem of the day is to check these three currents that are already pouring against the bulwarks of our peace and prosperity. To anchor the farmer to his land and the villager to his home; to enable him to till the land under equal conditions and to hold that home in independence; to save with his hands the just proportion of his labor, that he may sow in content and reap in justice, —this is what we need. The danger of the day is centralization, its salvation diffusion. Cut that word deep in your heart. This Republic differs from Russia only because the powers centralized there in one man are here diffused among the people. Western Ohio is happy and tranquil, while Chicago is feverish and dangerous, because the people diffused in the towns and the villages of the one are centralized and packed in the tenements of the other; but of all centralization that menaces our peace and threatens our liberties, is the consolidation of capital—and of all the diffusion that is needed in this Republic, congesting at so many points, is the leveling of our colossal fortunes and the diffusion of our gathered wealth amid the great middle classes of this people. As this question underruns the three tendencies we hast been discussing, let us consider it a moment.

Few men comprehend the growth of private fortunes in this country, and the encroachments they have made on the rest of the people. Take one instance: A man in Chicago that had a private fortune secured control of all the wheat in the country, and advanced the price until flour went up three dollars a barrel. When he collected $4,000,000 of this forced tribute from the people, he opened his corner and released the wheat, and the world, forgetting the famishing children from whose hungry lips he had stolen the crust, praised him as the king of finance and trade. Let us analyze this deal. The farmer who raised the wheat got not one cent of the added profit. The mills that ground it not one cent. Every dollar went to swell the toppling fortunes of him who never sowed it to the ground, nor fed it to the thundering wheels, but who knew it only as the chance instrument of his infamous scheme. Why, our fathers declared war against England, their mother country, from whose womb they came, because she levied two cents a pound on our tea, and yet, without a murmur, we submit to ten times this tax placed on the bread of our mouths, and levied by a private citizen for no reason save his greed, and no right save his might. Were a man to enter an humble home in England, bind the father helpless, stamp out the fire on the hearthstone, empty the scanty larder, and leave the family for three weeks cold and hungry and helpless, he would be dealt with by the law; and yet four men in New York cornered the world's cotton crop and held it until the English spindles were stopped and 14,000,000 operatives sent idle and empty-handed to their homes, to divide their last crust with their children, and then sit down and suffer until the greed of the speculators was filled. The sugar refineries combined their plants at a cost of $14,000,000, and so raised the price of sugar that they made the first year $9,500,000 profit, and since then have advanced it rapidly until we sweeten our coffee absolutely in their caprice. When the bagging mills were threatened with a reduced tariff, they made a trust and openly boasted that they intended to make one season's profits pay the entire cost of their mills—and these precious villains, whom thus far the lightnings have failed to blast, having carried out their infamous boast, organized for a deeper steal this season. And so it goes. There is not a thing we eat or drink, nor an article we must have for the comfort of our homes, that may not be thus seized and controlled and made an instrument for the shameless plundering of the people. It is a shame—this people patient and cheerful under the rise or fall of prices that come with the failure of God's season's charge as its compensation—or under the advance at the farm which enriches the farmer, or under that competitive demand which bespeaks brisk prosperity—this people made the prey and the sport of plunderers who levy tribute through a system that mocks at God's recurring rains, knows not the farmer, and locks competition in the grasp of monopoly. And the millions, thus wrung from the people, loaned back to them at usury, laying the blight of the mortgage on their homes, and the obligation of debt on their manhood. Talk about the timidity of capital. That is a forgotten phrase. In the power and irresponsibility of this sudden and enormous wealth is bred an insolence that knows no bounds. "The public be damned!" was the sentiment of the plutocrats, speaking through the voice of Vanderbilt's millions. In cornering the product and levying the tribute—in locking up abundant supply until the wheels of industry stop —in oppressing through trusts, and domineering in the strength of corporate power, the plutocrats do what no political party would dare attempt and what no government on this earth would enforce. The Czar of Russia would not dare hold up a product until the mill-wheels were idle, or lay an unusual tax on bread and meat to replenish his coffers, and yet these things our plutocrats, flagrant and irresponsible, do day after day until public indignation is indignant and shame is lost in wonder.

And when an outraged people turn to government for help what do they find? Their government in the hands of a party that is in sympathy with their oppressors—that was returned to power with votes purchased with their money—and whose confessed leaders declared that trusts are largely private concerns with which the government had naught to do. Not only is the dominant party the apologist of the plutocrats and the beneficiary of their crimes, but it is based on that principle of centralization through which they came into life and on which alone they can exist. It holds that sovereignty should be taken from the States and lodged with the nation—that political powers and privileges should be wrested from the people and guarded at the capital. It distrusts the people, and even now demands that your ballot-boxes shall be hedged about by its bayonets. It declares that a strong government is better than a free government, and that national authority, backed by national armies and treasury, is a better guarantee of peace and prosperity and liberty and enlightenment diffused among the people. To defend this policy, that cannot be maintained by argument or sustained by the love or confidence of the people, it rallies under its flag the mercenaries of the Republic, the syndicate, the trust, the monopolist, and the plutocrat, and strengthening them by grant and protection, rejoices as they grow richer and the people grow poorer. Confident in the debauching power of money and the unscrupulous audacity of their creatures, they catch the spirit of Vanderbilt's defiance and can aloud from their ramparts, "the people be damned!" I charge that this party has bought its way for twenty years. Its nucleus was the passion that survived the war—and around this it has gathered the protected manufacturer, the pensioned soldier, the licensed monopolist, the privileged corporation, the unchallenged trust—an whom power can daunt, or money can buy, and with these in close and constant phalanx it holds the government against the people. Not a man in all its ranks that is not influenced by prejudice or bought by privilege.

What a spectacle, my countrymen! This free Republic in the hands of a party that withdraws sovereignty from the people that its own authority may be made supreme—that fans the smoldering embers of war, and loosing among the people the dogs of privilege and monopoly to hunt, and harrow and rend, that its lines may be made stronger and its ramparts fortified. And now, it is committed to a crime that is without precedent or parallel in the history of any people, and this crime it is obliged by its own necessity as well as by its pledge to commit as soon as it gets the full reins of power. This crime is hidden in the bill known as the service pension bill, which pensions every man who enlisted for sixty days for the Union army. Let us examine this pension list. Twelve years ago it footed $46,000,000. Last year it was $81,000,000. This year it has already run to over $100,000,000. Of this amount Georgia pays about $3,500,000 a year. Think of it. The money that her people have paid, through indirect taxation into the treasury, is given, let us say to Iowa, for that State just equals Georgia in population. Every year $3,500,000 wrung from her pockets and sent into Iowa as pensions for her soldiers. Since 1865, out of her poverty, Georgia has paid $51,000,000 as pensions to Northern soldiers—one-sixth of the value of her whole property. And now it is proposed to enlarge the pension list until it includes every man who enlisted for sixty days. They will not fail. The last Congress passed a pension bill that Commissioner Black— himself a gallant Union general—studied deliberately, and then told the President that if he signed it, it would raise the pension list to $200,000,000, and had it not been for the love of the people that ran in the veins of Grover Cleveland and the courage of Democracy which flamed in his heart, that bill would have been law to-day. A worse bill will be offered. There is a surplus of $120,000,000 in the treasury. While that remains it endangers the protective tariff, behind which the trained captains of the Republican party muster their men. But let the pension list be lifted to $200,000,000 a year. Then the surplus is gone and a deficiency created, and the protective tariff must be not only perpetuated but deepened, and the vigilance of the spies and collectors increased to meet the demands of the government. And back of it all will be mustered the army of a million and a half pensioners, drawing their booty from the Republican party and giving it in turn their purchased allegiance and support.

My countrymen, a thousand times I have thought of that historic scene beneath the apple-tree at Appomattox, of Lee's 8000 ragged, half-starved immortals, going home to begin anew amid the ashes of their homes, and the graves of their dead, the weary struggle for existence, and Grant's 68,000 splendid soldiers, well fed and equipped, going home to riot amid the plenty of a grateful and prosperous people, and I have thought how hard it was that out of our poverty we should be taxed to pay their pension, and to divide with this rich people the crust we scraped up from the ashes of our homes. And I have thought when their maimed and helpless soldiers were sheltered in superb homes, and lapped in luxury, while our poor cripples limped along the highway or hid their shame in huts, or broke bitter bread in the county poor-house, how hard it was that, of all the millions we send them annually, we can save not one dollar to go to our old heroes, who deserve so much and get so little. And yet we made no complaint. We were willing that every Union soldier made helpless by the war should have his pension and his home, and thank God, without setting our crippled soldiers on the curbstone of distant Babylons to beg, as blind Belisarius did, from the passing stranger. We have provided them a home in which they can rest in honorable peace until God has called them hence to a home not made with hands, eternal in the heavens. We have not complained that our earnings have gone to pension Union soldiers—the maimed soldiers of the Union armies. But the scheme to rob the people that every man who enlisted for sixty days, or his widow, shall be supported at public expense is an outrage that must not be submitted to. It is not patriotism—it is politics. It is not honesty—it is plunder. The South has played a patient and a waiting game for twenty years, fearing to protest against what she knew to be wrong in the fear that she would be misunderstood. I fear that she has gained little by this course save the contempt of her enemies. The time has come when she should stand upright among the States of this Republic and declare her mind and stand by her convictions. She must not stand silent while this crowning outrage is perpetrated. It means that the Republican party will loot the treasury to recruit its ranks—that $70,000,000 a year shall be taken from the South to enrich the North, thus building up one section against another—that the protective tariff shall be deepened, thus building one class against another, and that the party of trusts and monopoly shall be kept in power, the autonomy of the Republic lost, the government centralized, the oligarchs established, and justice to the people postponed. But this party will not prevail, even though its pension bill should pass, and its pretorial God be established in every Northern State. It was Louis XVI who peddled the taxing privileges to his friends, and when the people protested surrounded himself with an army of Swiss mercenaries. His minister, Neckar, said to him: "Sire, I beseech you send away these Swiss and trust your people;" but the king, confident in his strength and phalanx, buckled it close about him and plundered the people until his head paid the penalty of his crime. So this party, bartering privileges and setting up classes, may feel secure as it closes the ranks of its mercenaries, but some day the great American heart will burst with righteous wrath, and the voice of the people, which is the voice of God, will challenge the traitors, and the great masses will rise in their might, and breaking down the defenses of the oligarchs, will hurl them from power and restore this Republic to the old moorings from which it had been swept by the storm.

The government can protect its citizens. It is of the people, and it shall not perish from the face of the earth. It can top off these colossal fortunes and, by an income tax, retard their growth. It can set a limit to personal and corporate wealth. It can take trusts and syndicates by the throat. It can shatter monopoly; it can equalize the burden of taxation; it can distribute its privileges impartially; it can clothe with credit its land now discredited at its banks; it can lift the burdens from the farmer's shoulders, give him equal strength to bear them—it can trust the people in whose name this Republic was founded; in whose courage it was defended; in whose wisdom it has been administered, and whose stricken love and confidence it can not survive.

But the government, no matter what it does, does not do all that is needed, nor the most; that is conceded, for an true reform must begin with the people at their homes. A few Sundays ago I stood on a hill in Washington. My heart thrilled as I looked on the towering marble of my country's Capitol, and a mist gathered in my eyes as, standing there, I thought of its tremendous significance and the powers there assembled, and the responsibilities there centered—its presidents, its congress, its courts, its gathered treasure, its army, its navy, and its 60,000,000 of citizens. It seemed to me the best and mightiest sight that the sun could find in its wheeling course—this majestic home of a Republic that has taught the world its best lessons of liberty—and I felt that if wisdom, and justice, and honor abided therein, the world would stand indebted to this temple on which my eyes rested, and in which the ark of my covenant was lodged for its final uplifting and regeneration.

A few days later I visited a country home. A modest, quiet house sheltered by great trees and set in a circle of field and meadow, gracious with the promise of harvest—barns and cribs well filled and the old smoke-house odorous with treasure—the fragrance of pink and hollyhock mingling with the aroma of garden and orchard, and resonant with the hum of bees and poultry's busy clucking—inside the house, thrift, comfort and that cleanliness that is next to godliness—the restful beds, the open fireplace, the books and papers, and the old clock that had held its steadfast pace amid the frolic of weddings, that had welcomed in steady measure the newborn babes of the family, and kept company with the watchers of the sick bed, and had ticked the solemn requiem of the dead; and the well-worn Bible that, thumbed by fingers long since stilled, and blurred with tears of eyes long since closed, held the simple annals of the family, and the heart and conscience of the home. Outside stood the master, strong and wholesome and upright; wearing no man's collar; with no mortgage on his roof, and no lien on his ripening harvest; pitching his crops in his own wisdom, and selling them in his own time in his chosen market; master of his lands and master of himself. Near by stood his aged father, happy in the heart and home of his son. And as they started to the house the old man's hands rested on the young man's shoulder, touching it with the knighthood of the fourth commandment, and laying there the unspeakable blessing of an honored and grateful father. As they drew near the door the old mother appeared; the sunset falling on her face, softening its wrinkles and its tenderness, lighting up her patient eyes, and the rich music of her heart trembling on her lips, as in simple phrase she welcomed her husband and son to their home. Beyond was the good wife, true of touch and tender, happy amid her household cares, clean of heart and conscience, the helpmate and the buckler of her husband. And the children, strong and sturdy, trooping down the lane with the lowing herd, or weary of simple sport, seeking, as truant birds do, the quiet of the old home nest. And I saw the night descend on that home, falling gently as from the wings of the unseen dove. And the stars swarmed in the bending skies—the trees thrilled with the cricket's cry—the restless bird called from the neighboring wood--and the father, a simple man of God, gathering the family about him, read from the Bible the old, old story of love and faith, and then went down in prayer, the baby hidden amid the folds of its mother's dress, and closed the record of that simple day by calling down the benediction of God on the family and the home!

And as I gazed the memory of the great Capitol faded from my brain. Forgotten its treasure and its splendor. And I said, "Surely here—here in the homes of the people is lodged the ark of the covenant of my country. Here is its majesty and its strength. Here the beginning of its power and the end of its responsibility." The homes of the people; let us keep them pure and independent, and all will be well with the Republic. Here is the lesson our foes may learn—here is work the humblest and weakest hands may do. Let us in simple thrift and economy make our homes independent. Let us in frugal industry make them self-sustaining. In sacrifice and denial let us keep them free from debt and obligation. Let us make them homes of refinement in which we shall teach our daughters that modesty and patience and gentleness are the charms of woman. Let us make them temples of liberty, and teach our sons that an honest conscience is every man's first political law. That his sovereignty rests beneath his hat, and that no splendor can rob him and no force justify the surrender of the simplest right of a free and independent citizen. And above all, let us honor God in our homes—anchor them close in His love. Build His altars above our hearthstones, uphold them in the set and simple faith of our fathers and crown them with the Bible—that book of books in which all the ways of life are made straight and the mystery of death is made plain. The home is the source of our national life. Back of the national Capitol and above it stands the home. Back of the President and above him stands the citizen. What the home is, this and nothing else will the Capitol be. What the citizen wills, this and nothing else will the President be.

Now, my friends, I am no farmer. I have not sought to teach you the details of your work, for I know little of them. I have not commended your splendid local advantages, for that I shall do elsewhere. I have not discussed the differences between the farmer and other classes, for I believe in essential things there is no difference between them, and that minor differences should be sacrificed to the greater interest that depends on a united people. I seek not to divide our people, but to unite them. I should despise myself if I pandered to the prejudice of either class to win the applause of the other.

But I have noted these great movements that destroy the equilibrium and threaten the prosperity of my country, and standing above passion and prejudice or demagoguery I invoke every true citizen, fighting from his hearthstone outward, with the prattle of his children on his ear, and the hand of his wife and mother closely clasped, to determine here to make his home sustaining and independent, and to pledge eternal hostility to the forces that threaten our liberties, and the party that stands behind it.

When I think of the tremendous force of the currents against which we must fight, of the great political party that impels that fight, of the countless host of mercenaries that fight under its flag, of the enormous powers of government privilege and monopoly that back them up, I confess my heart sinks within me, and I grow faint. But I remember that the servant of Elisha looked abroad from Samaria and beheld the hosts that encompassed the city, and said in agonized fear: "Alas, master, what shall we do?" and the answer of Elisha was the answer of every brave man and faithful heart in all ages: "Fear not, for they that be with us are more than they that be with them," and this faith opened the eyes of the servant of the man of God, and he looked up again, and lo, the air was filled with chariots of fire, and the mountains were filled with horsemen, and they compassed the city about as a mighty and unconquerable host. Let us fight in such faith, and fear not. The air all about us is filled with chariots of unseen allies, and the mountains are thronged with unseen knights that shall fight with us. Fear not, for they that be with us are more than they that be with them. Buckle on your armor, gird about your loins, stand upright and dauntless while I summon you to the presence of the immortal dead. Your fathers and mine yet live, though they speak not, and will consecrate this air with their wheeling chariots, and above them and beyond them to the Lord God Almighty, King of the Hosts in whose unhindered splendor we stand this morning. Look up to them, be of good cheer, and faint not, for they shall fight with us when we strike for liberty and truth, and all the world, though it be banded against us, shall not prevail against them.

Appendix B

Key Speeches of Tom Watson

Watson's Commencement Address At Mercer University

[Thomas E. Watson's "Commencement Address," presented at Mercer University, Macon, Georgia, 29 June 1886. The text is from Thomas E. Watson, *The Life and Speeches of Thomas E. Watson* (Nashville: The Author, 1908) 41-58.]

There is a spirit aboard which is born of suspicion, and nurtured by levity and cynicism. Its watchword is, Incredulity; its process, prejudiced inquiry; its results, skepticism. It sneers at devotion to duty, mocks at pretensions to the virtues, scouts the existence of any motives of action save the maxims of a narrow, unsympathizing selfishness. Its pleasure is to cast ridicule upon old accepted creeds; its pride of opinion flatters itself by the rejection of current beliefs; its levity harbors no respect for character, however exalted—for motive, be it never so pure; and no reverence for anything past or present, human or divine. Its disposition is unscrupulous and aggressive and malignant. Like the vulture, its circling search is for corruption; like the hyena, it digs up and devours what decency would hide and forget.

Ask of these thoughtful instructors what it is that disturbs them most in the contemplation of our future and I doubt not the answer will be that it is the spread of the empire of disbelief—an empire which preserves no temples sacred from attack—which has no Pillars of Hercules to mark the limit beyond which its vessels dare not sail.

I am not speaking of that skepticism which merely says, "I wish to fairly investigate and intelligently decide"—that skepticism which stops the approach of every creed or dogma, however ancient and revered, and claims the right to examine its passports ere it be permitted to cross the frontiers of belief. Such skepticism is worthy of all praise and the world is in its debt. Such skepticism broke the spell of old barbaric creeds and gave us intellectual growth, political freedom—shattered the chains of superstition and gave to a higher civilization the blessings of religious liberty. All honor to such skeptics. Philosophy claims them in Galileo and Newton; statesmanship in Mirabeau and Burke and Jefferson—religion in Luther and Calvin and Knox.

The skeptic I do mean is he who has run this habit of candid research into the abuse of indiscriminate disbelief. Who doubts because he thinks it displays great knowledge of the world and great mental superiority to doubt. Who doubts because he hears other doubt, because it is the fashion to doubt. Those who believe everything he considers to be fools—and he drifts among those who believe nothing—forgetting that they may be still bigger fools. Green being the color of the glasses he wears—all that he sees is green. He detects the mote in the eye without ever beholding the eye. The sun is to him all spots and eclipse—not a blazing light that leads the march of the universe. You'll hear his voice wherever you go. The history of the country is rife with his slanders and suspicions; its literature soiled by his satires and his ribaldry, his immoralities; the very music of the land, white-winged bird of Paradise that it is—desecrated and debased by the burden of his obscenities—his endless and shameless unbelief.

In history this man pulls down the idols we were used to worship and says "Lo, they are of clay." In theology he strips from the altar the creed of a thousand years and says, "You have no God." In this life around you he says of your courts, "They sell justice": of your laws, "They oppress the weak": or your rulers, "They are a defilement to their high places": of your press, "It prostitutes its power."

He appeals to the records of the race, to current affairs, finds instances of baseness, finds currents of crime and proclaims that all men have their price and the world is saturated with depravity.

Let us examine the accusation. Let us call for a copy of the indictment and a list of the witnesses. What does the skeptic charge and what can he prove?

He says human nature is pitilessly cruel and unjust. He proves by the record that children murder parents—that parents strangle children; that wives betray and poison husbands, that husbands beat and desert and assassinate wives. They prove that heirs-at-law fight like jackals around the deathbed of wealth, frantic for the spoils: that unrewarded honesty trudges dusty highways with bleeding footsteps—while thrifty rascality speeds by in parlor cars; that opulence moves luxuriously in trappings of silk and purple and fares sumptuously in palace halls; while beggary creeps with unavailing cry under the hedgerow and starvation stiffens that gaunt limbs to quietude and sleep.

He says it is shamelessly treacherous and he asks you to name a cause that had no traitor. He says that it sold the secret of the pass at *Thermopylae* and gave to its enemies the attempt to band together the tribes in one great effort for home and country: that it struck down Wallace on the Scottish hills; Pompey on the Egyptian beach, Darius in his Persian camp; King Philip—the grandest of Indians—in his forest retreat; that it bore a hand in the spoliation of Poland and Hungary; betrayed for British bribes the Home Rule of Ireland; made barter upon the liberties for which America was struggling, and feasted upon the necessities and humiliation of our own South.

He says it is venal and will sell for a price anything it ever possessed. That men have sold their convictions—their country—their kings —their God. That the Circassian will sell his son for the army—his daughter for the harem, that the soldier will sell his valor and his blood—the priest his prayers and absolution—the patriot the cause for which he bleeds.

Fearful indictment—horrible details. No wonder the weak bend to the tide and make up their belief from exceptions rather than rules—from instances of bad rather than from generalities of good.

For the sake of argument let us admit the whole thing. Let us admit that all men are vicious and corrupt—blot virtue from the earth, Jehovah from the sky, and where are we? What do we believe? That around the sacred hearth of home is no chaste affection—no devout joy; no innocence—love and peace: that around the circle of those we call friends is no real kindness, no true honor, no stanch loyalty; that beyond the evening and the stars is no Elysian field of light, but at the eye of this three-score and ten with all its struggles and sufferings, its hopes and fears, is simply and solely the nothingness and horror of the tomb. Great God! What a creed! How can it make us better or nobler to believe it? What can it do but chill the fervor, blight the hopes and darken the landscape of life?

Accept the logic of the position. Admit that honor's a myth, truth a dream, friendship a deception, love a sensuality and it does seem to me that the Evil Spirit of the world could but whisper in your ear his old-time advice "Curse God and die." And the sooner a believer in such a creed accepted the latter part of the advice, the better it would be for the rest of us. The belief is a faithful mirror to those who embrace it—to the men who believe evilly because too often they seek an evil creed to fit an evil life. They get an idea that the world is a sea where the big fish eat the little fish and that the only way to escape being devoured is to devour all others, and grasping, therefore, they must snatch. All others cheat, therefore they must swindle. And thus you see how scoundrels may be manufactured out of the plain principles of self-defense. Their motto is the phrase which Dickens puts into the mouth of Jonas Chuzzlewit: "Do others for they would do you." Appropriate motto from an appropriate source—a wretch who poisoned his father, broke the heart of his wife, lived in rascality, died in suicide. Give us the man who denies integrity and proclaims all men dishonest, and we have a knave who, if you give him half a chance, will steal the gold plugs out of your teeth. Give us the man who says all men are liars and we have Munchausen who never tells the truth except when it is necessary to give his tongue a rest from the monotony of lying.

What right have such creatures to infect the air we breathe and sit in judgment upon better men? Listen to the evidence of the drunkard and all men are tipsy—to the libertine putrid and foul and false, who never made a vow he didn't break, never received a trust he didn't betray—listen to him and the spotless robe of purity which womanhood wears and the angels might envy, lives only in the dream of youth, colors only the page of romance.

Such is the skeptic's creed. It has its followers everywhere who talk it, write it, live it. I have met them—you will meet them. Listening to them we doubt friends, distrust the family circle—lose faith in the possibilities of life. This creed I deny—this creed I scorn. This creed had I the power, I would stamp out from the face of the earth as I would the reptile that endangers our path.

What shall we believe? Weightier question will never strike your ear. Beliefs are the germs of principles: principles are the elements of manhood; and manhood, true, exalted manhood, is the summit of praiseworthy ambition. To constitute the highest type of manhood, we all agree that certain qualities are requisite; among them kindness, truth, honor, loyalty.

But do they exist? The skeptic says no, and listening to him we doubt where he doubts, reject what he rejects and turn a deaf ear to the call of our better nature.

Come! it's a grave matter. Comrades, let us examine it. Not in a spirit of levity. God forbid! The Caesar whom history shows you standing yonder at the Rubicon—march halted, legions silent, ponders upon a question no more serious to him than is this to you.

Is there no kindness? Look over all this globe and count if you can its aids to distress, its institutions of charity. Count the hospitals, the asylums, the orphanages, the homes for aged, infirm and needy. Trace them in city and town and country, on mountain and plain and desert; in zones frigid and temperate and torrid. Note the missions and the free schools. See every Government with its poor laws; every country with its pauper fund. See the very criminals jealously guarded from cruelty and want. How many nooks will you find where benevolence has not brought the charm of her presence—how many houses of mourning where she has not soothed aching heads and aching hearts—how many desert wastes where she has not planted and tended and nourished till barrenness blossomed into fruitfulness and beauty.

Kindness? Why its spirit is all-pervading and masterful. It melts the barriers and sectional coldness, ignores difference of race and color and condition; it overleaps the obstacle of distance and spans oceans and seas with its magic bridges. We read of the Federal soldier pensioned by a bountiful Government and not needing the pension, who seeks out some destitute and disabled Confederate and gives it to him. God pity them that they are so easy to find all through this Southern land!

We read that Senator Harris, of Tennessee, is providing place and means of livelihood to the family of Governor Brownlow, the man who denounced Harris, drove him from his country and put a price upon his head. Let us not forget that Brownlow before he died let kindness overcome cruelty and provided safety and comfort to Harris and the family of Harris.

Ireland is stricken with famine—Europe and America fill her empty homes with provisions. The North stands aghast at Chicago burnt, and the flames leap down from the woods around the Lakes and Wisconsin and Michigan are black with ruined homesteads. The South forgets abuse and slander and oppression and from out her own poverty she has kindness to divide with the suffering. The South is borne down by pestilence and her sick lie helpless in every city. The North forgets rancorous dislike, and the kindness of her aid and the reality of her sympathy did more to warm back into the Southern heart the Stars and Stripes than everything else since Appomattox.

The fire ball startles the sleeping city and it awakes to terror and danger and destruction. Let history make record of what is done there: generous courage, daring kindness; property saved, lives snatched from the very flames—a record braver and grander than ever blazoned a battlefield.

The storm comes thundering down the coast with bleakness of cloud, terror of wind and fury of foaming wave and the trembling vessels flee in horror. But the night was never yet so bleak or the tempest dread that heroism did not brave the peril and risk life to save life.

The pestilence steals into your city, driving away peace and joy and health. It drapes your houses in black, fills your beds with the sick—the hearses with the dead. It empties your streets and drives traffic from your gates—traffic no matter how lustful it is for gain; but in never yet has driven away those gentle sisters of mercy, Protestant as well as Catholics, who search for the suffering, watch at the bedside, soothe in the death agony and give health and time and life in the ministration of a divine compassion.

Is there no truth? You know the Psalmist, exclaimed: "I said in my haste that all men are liars;" and you remember the good brother who added, "Yes, and if David has taken all his life to think about it he would have reached the same conclusion." In one sense of the word I suppose we all do lie. For instance, you tell me you are sorry to hear that I have been sick, when the truth is you don't care any more about my health than you do about the fate of a last year's May pop.

I am sitting in my room on Sunday; have done a hard week's work and now I'm going to have a quiet, restful day at home—stretched on a lounge with a book in my hand. All at once a buggy drives up and stops at my gate. There's Jones and Jones' wife, who is as full of weak conversation as the church is of weak members; and Jones' baby, which is teething and giving its attention to the development of a fine, brave pair of lungs. The whole concern has come to spend the day! Merciful heavens! Seeing them coming in I grow faint and desperate and suicidal. I form wild notions of jumping over the back fence and taking to the woods. Too late. The door bell rings, and I sadly lay aside book and go to meet them. See me do it. "Why, Jones, old fellow, how d'ye do; and the Madam and the baby. Come in; come in—rejoiced to see you," and such a smile as I do get up. Well, now since I think of it, I am not so sure about this smiling business. If I am not a candidate for anything I am not so sure that I smile. If I am, I am quite as sure that I do. For when I'm a candidate I am like the balance of them and I have a lovely, heart-searching, vote lifting smile that my friends say is enough to melt the horns off a billy goat.

The reporter for the "Society Column" alludes to his lady friend as the "beautiful and accomplished" when he knows that her face is a howling wilderness of bone and freckles and things and that her mind is as empty as a politician's promise.

We members of the Bar have to examine applicants for admission. We ask them certain questions as to the law and they answer or don't answer, as the case may be, and we rise, address the Judge and say: "We are satisfied, your Honor." Sometimes we are called upon to examine one of these fellows who miss about four-thirds of all the questions we ask. Still we use the formula: "We are satisfied," and thus we let in another lawyer to ornament and bless mankind. And so we are satisfied—satisfied that he doesn't know the difference between a conditional Est and a gatling gun, satisfied that what he thinks he knows would stall a freight train on a down grade and what he *does* know wouldn't embarrass the retreat of a wounded mosquito.

The late Judge McLaws was one of the most courteous of men. Upon one occasion he was a member of the committee which examined an applicant at Waynesboro. The applicant belonged to the class of which I have been speaking: his brain was as sharp as a roll of butter and as strong as boarding house coffee, and as clean as the noonday mud. Judge McLaws asked him this question, that question and the other question. With a beautiful regularity he missed them all. Things were getting squally. Even Judge McLaws didn't feel that it would do to let him in without his answering at least one. But a brilliant idea struck the Judge, flashed upon him like sunbeams out of a cloud. He said to the applicant: "Mr. Brown, I believe your mother was a Miss Hawkins, wasn't she?" Brown says, "Yes." And McLaws rises with a smile that is seraphic and says: "I am satisfied, your Honor."

But these things ar trifles—denominated "White Lies." They spring from motives which do us no discredit—from a desire to add to the pleasantries, courtesies and amenities of social intercourse.

But the liar we mean he who falsifies knowingly, upon a matter material, with a motive as black as his words. You will find them in every community, but you will also find that they are few, isolated and held in contempt. The perjurer in all countries stands apart, branded, pilloried, towering in the eminence of his infamy. The ostracism to which he is condemned shows that his crime is unusual and shocks the moral sense of humanity.

I wish I had the time to enlarge upon this topic and show you what part truth plays in the drama of the world: to impress upon you that truth is the basis of the fame of painter and sculptor, orator and poet, statesman and philosopher: that institutions and laws, principles and creeds, die, with the day or outlive the centuries just in proportion as they conform to or are opposed by the resistless power of truth. In the brief space allotted to me I can only give you the suggestions, follow them with candid reflection and you will reach the conclusion that I most conscientiously hold—that so long as the divinity of good bears down and subjects the fiendishness of evil just so long will truth keep her foot upon the neck of falsehood.

Is there no honesty? What is it that holds together the business and commerce of the world—the vast web and woof of barter and exchange, export and import? What is it that gives to verbal promise the weight of gold; and brings paper into equality with coin and houses and lands? Why do we entrust the savings of a lifetime to bonds not due for ten or twenty or forty years? Why insure, depositing in bank, invest in stocks? Why create agents, trustees, executors or guardians? Why should the present redeem the pledges of the past as it does? Why should the present confide in the honor of the future as it does? I see from the papers that the Government of France asked for a loan on long time, at three per cent, of nine hundred million francs. The people in response have offered two billion seven hundred million. In other words, the citizen of France, living in a troublous present, knowing that times may change and the Government change, is yet willing to put himself, his fortune and his family in the keeping of the honesty of the future. One bank cashier defaults and scoots for Canada and we cry out "Depravity! Depravity!" We forget the ten thousand cashiers whose integrity is and will be as unshaken as a rock. A dozen politicians get smirched in some Broadway railroad swindle, some Yazoo fraud. Again our lamentations rise and we deplore the villainy which seems to stalk like a Leper, through public life crying, "Unclean! Unclean!" We forget the countless hundreds of those whose walk, even through the mire of politics, is so lofty that friends admire and enemies dare not assail.

But what Republican would be so blind in hatred as to deny honesty to Stephens and Toombs, Lamar and Davis? On the other hand what Democrat would feel that he did justice to the candor of his nature if he did not bear testimony to the worth of Lincoln and Sumner, Conkling and Phelps? Their names are synonyms of integrity—their records without stain. And when we see honesty so conspicuous that even among the politicians its presence is unquestioned, we feel as we do when we see the lilies lifting white faces from puddles, or violets shrinking amid bramble —we feel that the seeds of beauty have been so bountifully scattered by the hands of a gracious Providence that they bloom in spite of obstacles.

You see the vast fortune of the Rothschilds: you trace it to its source as you would the Mississippi—the Monarch of Rivers. We start from the magnificent outlet and move on up stream. We pass the Ohio bringing royal tribute, the Missouri with its muddy tide, the Illinois, the Wisconsin, the St. Croix, the Swan. We follow along the lessening stream, growing slender amid Northern woods—passing like a silver thread through a jeweled circlet of lakes, and our pleasure is but the deeper if we find the source of all the Mississippi's grandeur, of all its length and breadth and power, to be some lucid spring in sylvan shade, some crystal surface of Itasca Lake.

With like interest we trace to its source the wealth of the Rothschilds —wealth colossal, overshadowing Europe. We pass its tributaries here, its additions there—its loans for peace or war, its discounts for the Old World or the New—and away back in the dimness of the past it moves us with pleasure to see its slender beginning flowing from a source as pure as the waters from the rocks. Go read the story—the narrative of troublous times—of treasure entrusted to a Rothschild—of the Rothschild wrecked in the Revolution, property gone—home desolate but his trust kept secure—inviolate. Read it—remember it, and say with me that it gives to the name and the race a title of nobility higher and more enduring than the patent Victoria signed.

No honesty? Why, the veriest knave that ever wore a stripe—in his heart of hearts believes in its existence—and so does the rankest skeptic that ever polluted the air he breathed. Let disbelief in honesty really take possession of the world for one moment and the business of mankind halts! The great loom of traffic weaves no more. The great ocean of commerce checks its currents, calls in its tides and a Dead Sea is before you; and around us, in place of town and village and city, is the silence and emptiness of the desert. Your Black Fridays come—your panics of '73 with the terror of the cyclone and the rumbling of the earthquake. The markets of the world tremble and smite their knees in abject dismay. Commercial houses topple, banks crash, values shrink, securities vanish, stocks melt and through the consternation and the gloom come the cries of distress from men and women and children.

Why? Because, for one brief moment skepticism snatched the helm; doubt became pilot: and no sooner did he touch the wheel than the vessel dashed straight for the breakers, for ruin and for death.

Let confidence return! Let it come as the Master came that time the storm tossed the Sea of Galilee. And the tempest grows mute in the presence of its God, the sinking Peter rises to the surface and the rescued vessel, snatched from its peril, is safe on a tranquil sea!

Is there no loyalty? What is loyalty? To cling to those we love in shadow as in sunshine; to meet the duties of the hour ungrudgingly, unreservedly; to be as stanch to principle in defeat as well as in triumph: to follow the beck of duty, the demands of honor, the dictates of truth, the promptings of affection not only when to obey them may mean the grateful sound of applause, the chaplet of renown, the meed of pleasure or riches or office, but also when it may mean pain and censure and ridicule and dislike; when it means loss of favor, of friends, of riches, of the coveted boon of success. This is loyalty! Nay, it is more. It is the perfection of a sublime manhood which the very heavens must respect and all eternity reward.

Does it exist? The skeptic says, "No—most assuredly, no!"

Let us see: let us challenge the record! Let us call forth the heroes of the old time to confront and abash the pygmies of the new.

Do we not read of Ellen Douglas—who ran her bare arm through the hasps of the door through which assassins would come upon her king— did she not hold them all at bay till the tender flesh and bone was bruised and mangled and bleeding and the monarch had made his escape?

Do we read of Sir Philip Sydney lying on battlefield wounded to the death, his lips parched with thirst and yet true to the chivalrous teaching, refusing the cup of water because an unknown comrade lying there had necessities greater than his?

Did not every man and woman in the Highlands know that king's ransom was the price offered for the secret of the hiding place of the young prince, Charles Edward Stuart? Did not all know where that hiding place was; were not they all destitute—harassed by war—hounded by rapine on account of this very prince and did not they all, from the nobleman down to the churl, hold themselves aloof in contemptuous scorn from the bribe that England had offered?

The private soldiers capture Andre, and the wealthy young officer, horrified at his impending doom, offers purse and watch and unlimited promise for his freedom. Catch and hold in thy chalice, O muse of history, the golden reply: "We are poor men and needy, but all the wealth of England can't buy us."

No loyalty? No self-sacrifice for principle? Turn, O carping skeptic, back to the days of Christian persecution—gaze into the arena of Rome and see the lustful greed of the thousands gathered there in the power and pomp and insolence of their empire to gloat upon the helpless agony of martyrs. See them throw to the famished lion and ravenous tiger the followers of the Nazarene. "Renounce the God and live," shout the Romans. "No," answers strong manhood. "No," replies weak womanhood. "Rather will we cling to our God and die." And they cling to their God and die—torn limb from quivering limb amid the taunts and jeers of a heartless people.

No loyalty? Ah, flippant scoffer, who from the mole-hill of your own nature denieth the existence of the mountains on whose summits the clouds may love to linger, go and search and ponder and be ashamed. Uncover thy head when thou standest upon the soil where frail humanity chose death rather than surrender of conviction, grow reverent for once in thy life when thou seest the stakes at which it was burned, the rack on which it was tortured, the dungeons where the visionary horrors of hell were flung into the actualities of life.

Nay, go further. See all Holland ravaged by fire and sword for years and years and years when one word of apostasy would have brought relief. See the fairest provinces of Italy blackened and blasted by remorseless Alva. See the Huguenot loyal to faith—though it meant banishment from peace and plenty in sunny France to strife and privation in the forests of America; the Puritan, faithful to belief though it meant leaving of home and friends in quiet England to dangers of the sea, struggles with the savage and peril of starvation in the frozen wilds of the North.

View all this and if loyalty be still denied—loyalty sublime and complete—it is because the blindest of the blind is the man who *will not* see.

Loyalty? It is not the soul of domestic life, and is it not there what salt is to the sea, what the sun is to the flower? Does the skeptic deny its existence there? On the other hand, like the bluebells and the daisies, is it not so common that we cease to remark it? The Rosamond or Gabrielle or Magdalene goes into canvas, lives in poetry and song: a thousand vestals keep alight the scared fires of purity, noted only by those among whom they live. A Poppaea or Borgia murders or betrays a husband and history makes a monument to her shame: all through this land and other lands, through these times and all other times, are found faithful companions—who bear and forbear, who trust and keep trust and serve duty as faithfully as the rivers serve the sea.

What is the narrative of our domestic life? So ancient, so universal, we term it "The old, old story." Pardon me for one touch of its timeworn but sacred leaves.

Here's the maiden—in the glow of buoyant youth: queenly in the regalia gems of the graces; witching in the splendor of a loveliness which canvas can never picture, marble never embalm; a loveliness that has its rainbow beauty in the varying hue of cheek, shifting radiance of eye, in the harmony of look and tone and motion. "She is a woman, therefore to be wooed," etc.

She is wooed and is won. Happy the youth! Wooed, let us say, under the mystic spell of night, made up of starlight vague and dreamy, or fragrance faint from sleeping flowers, of melody pensive in some muffled murmur of brook, some distant note of bird.

Wooed and won! Lover and lady; groom and bride; husband and wife. Youth goes—is gone. Ah, that its stay is so brief!

Moonlit nights are gone, stern days of reality have come. Hot sunshine, weary road, toilsome tasks, heavy burdens; wear and tear and fret and strife. The bride no longer touches soft guitar or pens still softer verses. You may see her yonder in the back porch mending a hole in little Johnnie's trousers, or washing the greens for the dinner pot: if you drop in a chat awhile she has various remarks to offer relative to the cut worms which have taken a voracious fancy to her garden, and about her neighbor's chickens which she fears will drive her raving distracted. The gallant groom no longer dreams of the Ideal and pants for the Unattainable. You'll see him yonder at the lot counting the number of pigs the speckled sow has got. Step over to where he is and he'll argue with emphasis and feeling the problem as to whether or not sandy land is best for potatoes; and whether the "free nigger" is a success; and whether a religious man can plow a mule in a new ground without the whole team falling from grace.

Romance gone? Yes, every bit of it. Love gone? No—a thousand times no. Beneath that shingle roof is the glory of manhood, womanhood, wife leaning on the strong are found faithful, husband embalmed in affection unselfish, undoubting—wifely devotion which gives its tenderness to its king without measure, without murmur, as the ocean gives its moisture to the sun. Perfect trust, thankful content and the music of the gods—childhood's happy laughter. Clouds there have been in the domestic horizon. We can't deny it. The best of wives will sometimes forget to sew the buttons on, and put too much soda in the biscuit. But the very clouds have made the sunlight all the brighter. Discords there have been in the harp of home. We must frankly admit it. The best of husbands will sometimes bring company home on washdays and express himself a little too strongly about his mother-in-law. But the very discords have made the harmonies all the sweeter—harmonies, mark you, that are richer and softer and tenderer than the wreath of song which the mocking bird weaves around your midsummer night's dream.

Middle life passes—is gone. The children have married off and left them. The aged couple are again alone.

The old lady is an authority all over the whole neighborhood. If the pip breaks out among the chickens in three miles, she's consulted. All the mysteries of catnip tea are to her familiar as A B C's. She can make a poultice which will cure anything from the sting of a spider to the kick of a mule. She is almost glad when you are taken sick, so that she can come over with her knitting and her snuff and her motherly kindness and doctor you on root tea till you are up again.

As for the old man let us go up to his porch and hear him talk. He doesn't like these toothpick shoes the boys wear on their feet, nor the ivory-headed canes they stuff in their mouths—doesn't like this way of a young man's grabbing hold of a girl's arm and shoving her along as if she were a jackplane. He doesn't think they ought to raise hymns in church with a cornet—believes the old deacon can raise any hymn that's worth raising. Doesn't think his church needs a chandelier. Doesn't believe there's a single member of the congregation could play on it if they had one.

Dear old couple! Linked together by a thousand tender memories—loving now without passion but with an infinite peace and trust. Let us pause for a moment in the noisy hurlyburly of our lives and draw nearer to where they sit, for it seems to me I can hear something like this:

"John Anderson, may jo, John, when we were first acquent,
Your locks were like the raven's, your bonny brow was brent,
But now you're growing beld, John, your locks are like the snaw,

Yet blessings on your frosty pow, John Anderson, my jo.
"John Anderson, my jo, John, we clam the hill thegither,
And mony a canty day, John, we've had wi' ane anither;
Now we maun totter down, John, but hand in hand we'll go,
And sleep thegither at the foot, John Anderson, my jo."

Thus I have given you both sides of the question. Which will you take, by which of the two creeds will you live? It's a question you can't dodge, you've got to vote. It's a fence you can't straddle; you've got to light on one side or the other.

Upon the one hand are the men who have no faith—who tear down, rather than build up, slander rather than praise, injure rather than help, who deny to others the nobility of motive lacking in themselves, who make of this existence a cynic's corner to snarl in, and epicurean's paradise to repose in, or a sensualist's mire to wallow in.

On the other hand are the men with a creed and a purpose—men who see not only the darkness but the light, not only the thorn but also the beauty and fragrance of the rose, not only the deformities of vice but also the glories of virtue: men, earnest, straightforward, reverential men, who believe that this life of ours, throbbing with the passions and desires, thrilling with the knowledge of its power, infinite in the sweep of its aspirations, is not the plaything of a wanton's smile or a debauchee's lust, but is of all trusts the most sacred, of all opportunities the most sublime.

I address myself more particularly to the young gentlemen present. Comrades, this question is important to us beyond all other questions—life's race course stretches before us and we want to start right. And I say to you with all the earnestness of my nature, we can't afford to doubt. We can't afford to nourish that anxious wed called distrust. Have faith in your friend and you *may* lose him; doubt him and he is lost already. Have faith in the success of your undertakings and you may fail, doubt them and you had just as well make up your mind to do your wife's churning all your days. Adopt the nobler creed—for lofty beliefs are the seed beds of lofty achievement. Not only adopt it but live it. It can never lead us to shame or remorse or degrade us in feeling or position. It will ennoble us, lift us. It will lead us on to high aims and achievements. In success it will consecrate our glory—in defeat it will cheer us with a solace sweeter than any note that ever soften the throat of nightingale. A creed like this gives to history the deeds it loves to embalm—gave to the reverence of all ages the names of Hampden and

Sydney, of Grattan and Kossuth; made scared such fields as Bannockburn and Bunker Hill; put the light of immortality to burn forever where Bozzaris and Winkelried and Stonewall Jackson fell.

Be a man fashioned on this creed and the world will have need of you. What heroes did, you can do—meet the duties of your position. Everywhere is felt the want of earnest, honest, independent men—men with a purpose and firmness enough to pursue it; with principles and courage enough to retain them: men who belong to nobody, who are free from ring ownership and clique dictation; who scorn to be on a side simply because it's the winning side: men who stand erect in the plentitude of a royal manliness and think and believe and speak and act by the grand old principles of right!

Not that right merely which is synonymous with might, and success and temporary applause—but that higher and grander and better meaning of the term—right because conscience says the word, right because honor calls it so. What though such a course leads him to what the world call defeat? To such a man there's a question of character involved which overrides all mere clamor of failure or triumph. Such a man will walk down into the valley of the shadow of defeat and come forth with light of immortality on his face. Such a man becomes a Robert Emmet or a Robert Lee—whose graves are Mecca shrines where the patriotism of all countries makes devout pilgrimage and stands with head uncovered.

In the olden time the senate of his country voted to one of its generals the thanks of the commonwealth—not that he had won victories, not that he had brought home trophies—he had done neither; but because in an hour of peril and panic and disaster "he had not despaired of the Republic." Comrades, take the lesson home to your hearts. No matter what gloom spread itself about you keep the faith, be true to your creed. It will demand courage to do it--courage the most resolute and invincible. You will see vice prosper and increase; injustice prevail and spread. Friendship will meet you with betrayal; hope promise to delude; love itself smile on you to ensnare. Your heart will grow faint and droop and bleed, and when you see those on whom you built your trust banded with the enemies who would slay your peace, you will feel as Caesar felt when the knife of Brutus gleamed before his eyes. You fain would draw your mantle o'er your face and sink down to mute despair. But remember the brave example of the past and do not despond. Be loyal to the good old faith that makes the heroes; be loyal to the friend whose hand you clasp;

to the words that pass your lips; to the trust that binds your honor; to the duty which claims your devotion.

O comrade! Be earnest and brave and true! Leave trifling to those who have no aim—levity to those who have no faith. Be deaf to those who would wound you by their ridicule and jeers. Remember that the mockery was heard even while the sands drank the life blood of the martyr—while Calvary grew black in the death hour of a God. Be a man! Soiled by no bribe, daunted by no danger, cowed by no defeat and as sure as Jehovah lives and rules you will rank among those who give to this life of ours all of its sweetness, its glory and its joy!

Watson's Commencement
Address in Milledgeville, Georgia

[Thomas E. Watson's "Commencement Address," presented at Milledgeville, Georgia, June 1888. The text is from Thomas E. Watson, *The Life and Speeches of Thomas E. Watson* (Nashville: The Author, 1908) 59-73.]

A few years ago the novel-reading world was eagerly devouring the pages of that very curious book to which its author, Rider Haggard, had given the still more peculiar name of "She."

Those of you who may have read this story will remember the weird description of the landing of the English travelers on the savage coast of Africa; will remember how they found, imbedded in the mud, the ancient stone wharf; will remember how they toilfully made their way up the lonely river, labored through the long-forgotten canal and across the morass, to the people whose queen was "She-Who-Must-Be-Obeyed."

You will remember the description of the ruins of the City of Kor, but you will recall especially the pen picture of the deserted and crumbling Temple of Truth. Within its inner court stood a statue of the goddess whose worshipers had once filled that waste with their hurrying footsteps; whose voices had once filled that silence with sounds of devotion. Upon a pedestal stood a magnificent marble globe, and upon this globe stood a sculptor's dream of female loveliness. Its hands were extended in supplication, for a veil was over the face. There it stood, divine amid the desolation, silvered in the moonlight which softened while it illuminated every outline; and thus it had stood for ages—*Truth beseeching the world to lift her veil.*

In this symbol, sole remnant of the glories of the ruined temple, there is a profound meaning. The desolate city may lie about her, and the very precincts once peopled by her votaries may give place to brambles, but Truth herself is imperishable—survives all wreck and change; and if her prayer be slighted and her veil never lifted, the people perish while she survives.

During the hour allotted me to-day, I know of nothing better for me to do than to talk to these young men on the thoughts suggested by the veiled statue of Truth.

Be True.

If I were asked to sum up in one sentence the highest purpose which man can have in this life, I would say it was *"To seek the truth and to live it."*

Not only is this purpose a noble one, but it is one which is absolutely necessary to the true and permanent success of the individual or the mass; the citizen or the government. Creeds have lived or died, laws have been dominant or trampled on in exact proportion to the elements of truth which they contained. Apparent exceptions prevail, but they do so only in appearance, and the success of falsehood is, in the nature of things, bound to be partial and temporary. The constant tendency of the universe and all in contains is to conform to *the truth*.

The Philosopher.

The philosopher seeks the truth, and in proportion that he finds it, benefits mankind. Theories come and go, hypothesis chases speculation, and demonstration steps on the toes of surmise, but the constant effort is to find the truth. The church may stretch Galileo on the rack, the universities of Spain may solemnly denounce Sir Isaac Newton, but Truth marches on with serene power and extends her scepter over the bowed head of the world.

Boundless is the gratitude we owe to the philosophers. They brought reason to bear upon nature, expounded her meaning and explained away her mysteries. They robbed the eclipse of the terror which once sent the nations to their knees; severed famine and pestilence and earthquake from any connection with the wrath of God; established the uniformity and permanency of nature's laws, and hurled superstition from its throne in the minds and hearts of men.

Law and Government.

From a time ages in advance of Moses it has been the task of statesmen to write the law in conformity with truth. When they have done so their work has been immortal. A cardinal truth, once discovered, survived even the people who discovered it, and carried its precious freight, like another *Goodspeed*, across unknown seas to bless unborn people.

The Hindoos are a decayed nation—prostrate beneath British rule— but in their code of laws there were some regulations so wise, so just, so beautiful that they have made a circuit of the globe and have imbedded themselves in every system which deserves honorable mention. The laws, like the nations, have come from the East, and the Hindoo laws will out-live the race which framed them.

The Goths and the Vandals could beat down the frontier guards of the Roman Empire, sack its cities and divide its provinces, but they could not conquer its laws. Upon the other hand, if there is any special system of jurisprudence which may be said to govern the affairs of men to-day it is that of ancient Rome.

You will hear much said about the English common law. You will hear it praised as if it were some divinely inspired oracle. Don't believe a word of it. The English common law was the brutal code of half-naked savages. The truth was not in it and it fell. It deserves to fall. Under it a woman was serf and a poor man a slave. Its land tenure was infamous; its methods of trial were heathenish and idiotic; its punishments were revolting in their devilish cruelty.

Superstition hung like a pestilence on every principle of the "Unwritten" law of England. Some tyro, fresh from his Blackstone, will claim that the jury system is the pride of the common law.

The jury system had no existence until after the Norman conquest, and it was totally inefficient for general good until love of liberty, general intelligence and higher ideals left the old common law a stranded wreck.

Its principles, its purposes and its methods had to surrender because they were false—false to the true relation between government and people; between master and servant, between husband and wife; false to the true relation between innocence and guilt, between crime and punishment.

I do not mean to say that our code of to-day speaks the truth upon all subjects. It does not do so. But it is an immense improvement upon the code of one hundred years ago.

The Court.

When you go into one of those judicial mills called a court of justice, you may have these ideas weakened. You may find it difficult to remember that the law seeks the truth.

There is the judge, the fountainhead, the judicial guardian of the rights of the parties litigant. He is supposed to be an able man. He himself has no doubt upon that subject. He is supposed to be impartial, and the fact that he tries a railroad case with a free pass in his pocket (while the jury have none), does not for one moment shake his conviction that the jury is "prejudiced."

If a member of that jury accepts a five-cent cigar or a glass of red lemonade from lawyers or litigants, the verdict must be set aside—no matter how much expense it involves, no matter how little the cigar or the lemonade may have to do with the verdict. It becomes at once a self-evident fact that the jury did not surrender to law or evidence, but capitulated to the red lemonade.

But the judge on the bench, with no eleven associates to hold him in check, can quietly utilize a free pass worth hundreds of dollars, can serenely warn the jury not to have any bias or prejudice against the issuer of that free pass, and never once have his conscience ruffled by the thought that he is virtually in the position of the bribe-taker.

And his excuse is more shameful to the judiciary than his offense—"They all do it."

Consider, now, the lawyers. Not one of them wants justice done simply because it is justice. If my client happens to be right I want him to win, not so much because he is right as because he is my client. It is necessary to my reputation that he *should* win.

If the other side indulges in any tricks against my client, I am indignant; not so much because they are wrong as because they are injurious.

On the contrary, if my client is in the wrong, I cannot desert him. I dare not stand up in court and ask the judge to strike my name from the docket and thus retire from the case. The reproach of bench and bar and people would fall on me like an avalanche. I would never get another case. Once in, I must stay in. I must prop the falling cause. I must bull-rag the witnesses; I must abuse the other fellow; I must voraciously (if I can) eat up the lawyer on the other side; I must inflame the passion, prejudice or pity of the jury; I must confound and confuse the judge; and if there is a particularly truthful witness on the other side and his testimony is specially in my way, I must go for that witness with an appetite which will take no denial and no satisfaction. I must pound him and grind him. I must throw him up and fling him down. I must give him "cat o' nine tails" externally and aqua fortis internally. In other words, I must deface, disfigure and demolish this honest witness to such an extent that his neighbors on the jury will forget that he is a reputable citizen who has sworn the truth. And all this is done that my miserable scoundrel of a client may gain where he should lose, and that I may have the credit of winning where I should be defeated.

Suppose the witness appeals to the judge for protection? He will not get it. He will be told that he must not interrupt counsel. If he persists in his objection to the style in which I am tearing his reputation to tatters, and becomes unruly and demonstrative, his honor, the judge, will fine him for contempt of court. When the trial is over the judge and bar will compliment me on my splendid invective and the magnificent style in which I destroyed that truthful witness. The jury itself will enjoy the gladiatorship, and for years afterward will remember the witness, chiefly because of the cowardly attack which I made on him in a place where he could not defend himself.

Is not this a faithful picture of the court room which you may witness any day in this land?

Is it right? In God's name, are we not drifting away from the truth when our lands, liberty and life may depend on the speech of the advocate?

Reforms Needed.

For this state of affairs a remedy must be found. A trial in the court room must be made more of judicial examination by the judge and jury, and less of prize-fight between the lawyers.

The present system no longer serves its purpose. The public has lost confidence in it.

A system which sends a negro to the chain gang for betting a dime on "the first game of seven-up" and finds itself powerless to punish the stock gambler is weak unto rottenness, and there is no use denying it.

A system which tears a white tenant from his family and puts him in chains and stripes because he sells cotton for something to eat and leaves his rent unpaid, and which at the same time cannot punish its railroad kings who shamelessly violate the penal statutes, is a system which no honest man can heartily respect.

National Life.

The constant necessity of any government is to find the truth. Without it no real prosperity is possible.

I do not forget that error has frequently crystallized in the institutions of a country; but when it has done so ruin follows.

The unequal treatment of the classes, the unequal levying of the taxes, the unequal distribution of wealth have been three of the main causes which have peopled the cemeteries of the past with dead empires.

The French Revolution.

In France we find one illustration which will serve for many. All the power, privilege and wealth were centered in one class. The nobles and the priests constituted this dominant caste. Only they could hold office. Only they could reach promotion. They alone possessed wealth.

The nobility and the church owned most of the land. They drew enormous salaries and pensions and perquisites, but they contributed almost nothing to the support of the State. A peasant they despised. They could beat him, imprison him, outrage him in person, property, family, and he had no redress. He must give his labor to them without pay.

He must grind at the lord's mill; and if he wished the privilege of mashing his wheat between two rocks at home he had to pay for it. He must carry his grapes to the lord's press; his bread to the lord's oven. Five-eighths of his crop went to the tax-gatherer.

Only nobles could kill game. The peasant must allow wild boars to ravage his fields. He dare not kill them. That sport belonged to the noble.

He must allow troops of deer to trample down his crops. He could not kill one at the peril of his life! The sport was reserved for the noble.

Partridges must not be disturbed in their nests or in their feedings, nor must the peasant manure his crops while the young birds were growing up. It was thought to spoil their flavor, and this could not be endured by the noble.

Abuses so terrible, in some of the fairest provinces of France, crushed out cultivation entirely, and the country became a desert, while the cities were crowded with the starving peasants who had left them.

At the same time the church held property to the amount of four hundred million dollars, with a yearly revenue of fifteen million dollars, and did not pay one cent to tax.

This pitiless policy brought its natural result. The goose, being in a dying condition, yielded no more golden eggs. National bankruptcy came. The huge falsehood began to collapse.

The terrified king asked his minister what he must do. The minister said: "Compel the nobles and the priests to bear their equal share of taxation."

The monarch was delighted. He assembled the priests and the nobles. He said to them in effect: "Gentlemen, you have for ages monopolized the wealth and honors of this realm, and you have contributed little to the expenses of the Government. All the revenues of the Government go to you. The people get none of them. The people are starving and can pay no more. Hence, I ask you to allow your property to be taxed for the public weal."

What was the response? A cry of indignation which drove the minister from power and the king from his purpose. What was the result?

Revolution, red-handed, leaped upon the false order of things and swept it from the face of the earth.

I am sorry for the poor king who was beheaded, and for the poor queen also, but I am yet more sorry for the nameless poor who starved under misrule, and for those ragged wretches who were hanged at the palace gates because they had come there to ask for work and bread.

Dangers Ahead of Us.

We pride ourselves upon the equality guaranteed in the Declaration of Independence. The theory that before the law all men are equal is the glory of Jeffersonian Democracy. He believed with all his soul that classism, special privilege, concentrated power and corporate wealth were deadly enemies to this government. He was right. This government to-day has left the simple, majestic and true ideal of Jefferson, and has merged into the consolidated empire Hamilton desired.

The system is false and cannot live. It is glaringly untrue in theory and in practice, in outline and in detail. Judged by the Declaration of Independence it is false; judged by the Constitution it is false; judged by the republican spirit of this people it is false. And it will die just as certainly as there are enough brave men left to denounce the system and arouse the people to tear it to pieces.

If I were to go into detail to prove this I would be accused of making a political speech, where it is out of place. Therefore, I merely call your attention to these general facts: the tendency of the government to favor some industries at the expense of others; to favor some classes at the expense of others; to enforce general contributions from all the people when the benefit goes directly into the pockets of a few; to grant special privileges to some which it denies to others; to place the taxes almost entirely upon those least able to bear them; to relieve entirely from taxation those who derive the greatest benefit from the Government and who are most able to pay; aiding and encouraging the strong to oppress to weak— sanctioning the large fortune when it swallows the small one, and the large company when it gobbles up the little one; and fostering the trust which destroys or absorbs the independent enterprises that would stand against it.

Shameful system! Shameful Government which permits it. It is a burning lie before God and man, and God's omnipotence is pledged to the proposition that it cannot live.

Choice of Profession.

No question can be more absorbing at a commencement than this:

"What are these young people going to do?"

Young gentlemen, there is in every walk of life both truth and falsehood. Learn to know the one and love it. Learn to know the other and hate it.

Do you think of being a lawyer?

Few greater men have lived than really true lawyers. Few meaner men have ever lived than the false ones, and you can't shoot off a scatter gun in any given direction without crippling some of them.

The True Lawyer.

But the true lawyer, who is he? In ancient history he is the citizen who would travel on foot from land to land, endure every privation, incur every danger in order that he might study the laws, customs and manners of other people, and carry the best of it all back to his own people to improve them with it. He gave his life for his country in the strictest and noblest sense.

What profounder remark was ever made than this by Solon: "I have given my people not the best laws, but the best they were fitted to receive."

What grander man ever lived than the great Roman lawyer whom Nero commanded to justify that tyrant's murder of his mother? Lofty type of the loftiest ideal! We can see him yet, the grand figure of pagan manhood, through the mist of the ages, as he draws his mantle about him and goes to his death, rather than stain his hands with the ghastly work!

Go into France and find me the heroes who led her from feudalism to liberty; and when you crown each of them, it is a lawyer who wears your honors!

Cross the channel to England and seek among her illustrious dead those apostles of freedom, to whose memories you will bare your heads, and it is to a band of noble lawyers that you have uncovered!

Ask me to whom popular rights and the knowledge of how to enforce them is most to be credited during this century, and I answer without a moment's hesitation, Daniel O'Connell, the great Irish lawyer!

To him we owe the science of agitation; the irresistible but peaceable marshaling of public opinion to change customs, policies and laws; to him we owe the demonstration of the profound truth that reforms are not granted merely because they are right, but they are granted when it is no longer possible to refuse them.

Leaving the Old World and coming to the New, the same fact meets us. The signal fires of the Revolution were lit by lawyers; the Declaration of Independence was written by a lawyer—so the Constitution; and the man to whose doctrines of equality the people are returning now as fast as they can march was Thomas Jefferson, the lawyer. So much for the ornaments of our profession. I glory in its opportunities for good.

I never yet faced a jury where life, liberty and property were involved and wrong was threatened that I did not feel my breast swell—proud of the splendid privilege of being the champion of the right. Never such a trill enters my veins as when by some just verdict, I can send back to the old homestead, safe now for all time, the family who love it most, and to whom every feature of the landscape is festooned with tender memories; or give back to some drooping wife—weeping bitterly and fearfully amid her little ones shadowed by orphanage—the missing light —without which home would be always dark.

But of all mean creatures, deliver us from the lawyer who perverts truth, ferments discord, thinks only of his fee, tampers with witnesses and bribes jurors.

The lawyer who knowingly uses false testimony, knowingly misleads the judge, knowingly takes unjust advantage of the other side, has, in my humble judgment, done an unprofessional thing and made himself a party to a crime.

Young gentlemen, if you wish to be a lawyer, be one. It is a most honorable profession. But belong to the true and not to the false. If your client be guilty go no further than to hold the State to a strict proof of guilt. That far you may go in honor. Further you cannot go. Make yourself no accomplice in perjury or bribery. Remember that your client has not bought your character.

Avoid the narrowness which so often comes from regarding law as merely technical. Lift yourself to view it as the application of right to the relations between man and man.

Some of these days I pray that we may have in our courts and in our regulations less to technicality and more of the spirit of justice.

The Politician.

Do any of you think of being politicians?

I hope so. If there is anything which this country needs just now it is more politicians of—the right sort.

Henry Clay told his sons to "be dogs rather than politicians." He died a disappointed man; so did Webster; so did Calhoun. Why? Like children, they were eternally crying for the toys they couldn't get. They wanted, each of them, to be President, and it soured them when the "splendid misery" of that highest office passed them by.

But it does seem to me that the politician of the higher type is absolutely essential in all countries. Who is he, and what is his mission?

He is the citizen who loves justice in the laws; who believes that the doctrine of right should be the creed of government as well as of individuals. His mission is to denounce abuses and propose remedies; to oppose bad laws and to advocate good ones; to educate the masses of the people upon the true principles of government, to lead them an opposition of administrative wrongs; to embolden them to stand squarely for their guaranteed rights, to labor to the end that equity shall be preserved, that the avenues of promotion shall be kept open to all alike, and that the country shall be henceforth and forever a decent place for the people to live in—free from the tyranny of classes, free from the exactions of a moneyed aristocracy or an intolerant and corrupt priesthood; free from the legalized tyranny of capital over labor—of the rich over the poor.

Such is my conception of the true politician.

Now as to the false. You feel the need of a disinfectant when you approach him. He looks bad, he smells bad and he is bad. He is abroad in the land. The impudence of Satan is in his face, and the mainspring of his existence is "boodle." Principles are, to him, things to use, trade on and desert.

His fellow-man is to him either the hunters or the game—either the fellows he is after, or the fellows who are after him. The Government is the machinery which collects the fleece from the lambs; for that reason he loves the Government and goes after the fleece.

Truth, honor, patriotism are so many stage habits, which he may or may not assume, and put off as the occasion may require.

You will find him enthroned in every city. Generally he bosses the town. His co-partner is the saloon-keeper on the corner. Between them vice and fraud run rampant through the streets; taxes are high and thievery prevalent; jobbery of all sorts preys upon the city, and decent citizens get to the point where despair scarcely complains.

Do any of you wish to become politicians?

If so, avoid the false as you would a pestilence. Stand for the true, and after a while the people will understand you and appreciate you.

The people need you! Justice and good government need you! If the appeal moves you, come quickly, for time presses. If this country is to be rescued from the dominion of a foul plutocracy there is not a day to lose. Every hour makes our chains heavier and stronger. If I could send this feeble voice like a trumpet through all this land, through every walk, into every condition, its alarm would be: *"Rise up and strike your enemies! Your homes and your liberties are being lost!"*

The Farmer.

Do you think of being a farmer?

I hope some of you do, but I doubt it. There is no charm in agriculture now. The country mansions have gone to decay; the fields are worn to sand or seamed with gullies; the ditches in the low ground have filled, and the meadow, ah! the green, flower-scented meadow we children loved, has become a marsh.

The negroes have moved into the "big house." They have propped the chimney with a pole. They have mended the windows with guano sacks. A bag or two of Western corn lies on the piazza floor. Three yellow dogs sleep around the steps and only at drowsy intervals rouse up and remonstrate with the fleas. The white picket fence is gone. It made good kindling wood. The flower yard is gone—sacrificed to the old brindle cow.

And yet, once upon a time, the humming bird would leave its cool nest in the woods to come hither and linger hour by hour, sipping the sweets of the pinks and feasting upon the bosom of the imperial rose.

Once upon a time, little white maidens, pure as the lilies they loved, would gather here dainty offerings of courtesy, or of tenderness, and every blossom that bloomed was, by sacred association, a forget-me-not.

Gone is the orchard with its snow-drift of apple blossoms, its aroma of velvet peach; and the spring at the foot of the hill, where the melon used to cool, is choked with weeds; and the path which led to it has had no footsteps upon it this many a year.

Where are the "old familiar faces"? Gone. There was a mortgage; there was a lawsuit; there was a sheriff's sale.

This is the short and simple story of farm life in the South.

Ousted from the country, the family "broke up" and "moved to town."

That's the epitaph for a thousand dead farms in Georgia and elsewhere.

What drove them to town? The fact that it was well-nigh impossible to prosper in the country. The pitiless burden of unequal taxation, the impossibility of buying or selling except at other people's prices. A currency system which made the farmer and his lands an outlaw from its benefits; these and causes similar to these broke his fortune and broke his spirit—took his home and took his hopes.

This system is false and it shall die!

There shall be no peace and no truce until this foul outrage upon human rights is obliterated from the face of the earth.

A Plea for the Farm.

Young gentlemen, there is no grander work for patriotism than the upbuilding of rural life to its true dignity and usefulness and prosperity. If you are inclined in that direction, go, but go with a determination that the present false order of things must end, that you shall not be made a political pariah merely because you are a farmer; that your industry shall not be taxed to death in order that great fortunes shall be built up for other people. Demand of your rulers that the law shall treat your industries just as it treats others, equally as to burdens and equally as to benefits. I would that I could see the glory come back to Southern farms. I would that I could see gullied fields throw off the sedge and the briar, and take once more to their brown bosoms golden grain. I wish I could see the red June apple of old times hang in every orchard and could catch the tinkle of the cow bell in every meadow.

I wish I could see the old folks come back from town, re-shingle the "big house" and reset the flower yard. I wish that I could see every old parlor rehung with the family pictures, and the weeds and grass cleared away from the graves of those who sleep under the trees in the garden. Would that this country could be built up again, and built up by those who love it most.

Many a time have I walked from field to field on my old farm, my ears filled with the "drowsy hum of bees," while cattle were browsing lazily on the green grass, the spring branch gurgling down the meadow —and mocking-birds sending rapturous melody through the summer woods—and I would say to myself: "There can be no better land than this. In earth and sky and water is life and light and fruitfulness. To redeem this heritage were a holy work—to people these solitudes and bring back to darkened homes the contentment and the plenty which by right is theirs."

A great pity swells within me for the toil-worn faces I see in these country lanes and ragged fields—many of them poor old veterans who fought with Lee, and who never knew how cruel man could be to man till they came and began the battle with poverty.

Legislator! Study the condition of this people, and out of your mercy grant them justice!

Editors! You who lead public opinion! Go among these people and count the wounded, the dying and the dead, on the field where they fell, and you will return to your sanctum instructed and chastened, and never again will you mete out to them or their cause your doubts, your scorn or your abuse.

Unveil the Truth.

Some traveler of the future may strike this coast and find it a morass, as Rider Haggard's traveler found Africa. He may wander at mud-covered wharves, make painful way along forgotten canals, penetrate to wasted interiors where our civilization exists in vague tradition, may muse around the ruins of our great cities and wander curiously into the deserted temples—but if so, the cause will be easy to trace. The worshipers of Truth will have left her sanctuaries, and the glorious statue which represents her will be yet standing in the midst of her silent court—with the hands yet beseeching and the veil yet upon her face.

Selected Bibliography

Tom Watson, Henry Grady, And Southern Oratory

A. Books

Arnett, Alex Mathews. *The Populist Movement in Georgia.* New York: Longmans, Green and Co., 1920.

Boase, Paul, editor. *The Rhetoric of Protest and Reform: 1878-1898.* Athens: Ohio University Press, 1980.

Braden, Waldo W. *The Oral Tradition in the South.* Baton Rouge: Louisiana State University Press, 1983.

Braden, Waldo W., editor. *Oratory in the New South.* Baton Rouge: Louisiana State University Press, 1979.

Brewton, William W. *The Life of Thomas E. Watson.* Atlanta: The Author, 1926.

Brigance, William Norwood, editor. *A History and Criticism of American Public Address.* New York: McGraw-Hill, 1943.

Cash, W. J. *The Mind of the South.* New York: Vintage Books, 1969.

Clark, Thomas D. *The Emerging South.* New York: Oxford University Press, 1968.

Davis, Harold E. *Henry Grady's New South: Atlanta, A Brave and Beautiful City.* Tuscaloosa: University of Alabama Press, 1990.

Degler, Carl N. *Place Over Time: The Continuity of Southern Distinctiveness.* Baton Rouge: Louisiana State University Press, 1977.

Eaton, Clement. *The Growth of Southern Civilization.* New York: Harper and Row, 1961.

Foster, George M. *Ghosts of the Confederacy:Deafeat, the Lost Cause, and the Emergence of the New South 1865 to 1913.* New York: Oxford University Press, 1987.

Gaines, Francis Pendleton. *Southern Oratory: A Study in Idealism.* Tuscaloosa: University of Alabama Press, 1946.

Gaston, Paul M. *The New South Creed: A Study in Myth-Making.* Baton Rouge: Louisiana State University Press, 1976.

Goodwyn, Lawrence. *The Populist Moment.* London: Oxford University Press, 1978.

Grady, Henry W. *The New South and Other Addresses.* New York: Charles E. Merrill, 1904.

Harris, Joel Chandler, editor. *Life of Henry W. Grady.* New York: Cassell Publishing, 1890.

Harris, Nathaniel E. *Autobiography: The Story of an Old Man's Life with Reminiscences of Seventy-Five Years.* Macon GA: J. W. Burke Company, 1925.

Hicks, John D. *The Populist Revolt.* Lincoln: University of Nebraska Press, 1961.

Hill, Samuel S., editor. *Religion and the Solid South.* Nashville: Abingdon Press, 1972.

Hobsen, Fred. *Tell about the South: The Southern Rage to Explain.* Baton Rouge: Louisiana State University Press, 1983.

Holland, DeWitte, editor. *America in Controversy: A History of American Public Address.* Dubuque IA: William C. Brown, 1973.

Holland, DeWitte, editor. *Preaching in American History.* Nashville: Abingdon Press, 1969.

Kwiat, Joseph J. and Mary C. Turple, editors. *Studies in American Culture: Dominant Ideas and Images.* Minneapolis: University of Minnesota Press, 1960.

Lane, Mills, editor. *The New South: Writings and Speeches of Henry Grady.* Savannah: The Beehive Press, 1971.

Logue, Cal M. and Howard Dorgan, editors. *A New Diversity in Contemporary Southern Rhetoric.* Baton Rouge: Louisiana State University Press, 1987.

Logue, Cal M. and Howard Dorgan, editors. *The Oratory of Southern Demagogues.* Baton Rouge: Louisiana State University Press, 1981.

Nixon, Raymond B. *Henry W. Grady: Spokesman for the New South.* New York: Alfred A. Knopf, 1943.

Olmstead, Clifton. *History of Religion in the United States.* Englewood Cliffs NJ: Prentice-Hall, 1960.

Osterweis, Rollin G. *The Myth of the Lost Cause: 1865-1900.* New York: Archon Books, 1973.

Osterweis, Rollin G. *Romanticism and Nationalism in the Old South.* New Haven: Yale University Press, 1949.

Pollack, Norman. *The Populist Mind.* Indianapolis: Bobbs-Merrill Co., 1967.

Savage, Henry. *Seeds of Time: The Background of Southern Thinking.* New York: Henry Holt and Company, 1959.

Shaw, Barton C. *The Wool-Hat Boys: Georgia's Populist Party.* Baton Rouge: Louisiana State University Press, 1984.

Shurter, Edwin DuBois, editor. *The Complete Orations and Speeches of Henry W. Grady.* Norwood, Massachusetts: Norwood Press, 1910.

Smith, Stephen A. *Myth, Media, and the Southern Mind.* Fayetteville: University of Arkansas Press, 1985.

Tindall, George B. *Romance and Realism in Southern Politics.* Athens: University of Georgia Press, 1961.

Watson, Thomas E. *Bethany: A Story of the Old South.* New York: D. Appleton and Company, 1904.

Watson, Thomas E., editor. *History of Southern Oratory.* Volume 9 of *South in the Building of the Nation.* Richmond VA: Southern Publication Society, 1909.

Wilson, Charles Reagan. *Baptized in Blood: The Religion of the Lost Cause: 1865-1920.* Athens: University of Georgia Press, 1980.

Woodward, C. Vann. *Origins of the New South: 1877-1913.* Baton Rouge: Louisiana State University Press, 1951.

Woodward, C. Vann. *Thinking Back: The Perils of Writing History.* Baton Rouge: Louisiana State University Press, 1986.

Woodward, C. Vann. *Tom Watson: Agrarian Rebel.* London: Oxford University Press, 1938.

B. Articles

Braden, Waldo W. "Myths in a Rhetorical Context." *Southern Speech Communication Journal* 40 (Winter 1975): 133-126.

Braden, Waldo W. "Southern Oratory Reconsidered: A Search for an Image." *Southern Speech Communication Journal* 29 (Summer 1964): 303-15.

Braden, Waldo W. "The Rhetoric of a Closed Society." *Southern Speech Communication Journal* 45 (Summer 1980): 333-51.

Bryan, Ferald J. "Henry Grady and Southern Ideology: An Analysis of the Texas State Fair Address." In *Rhetoric and Ideology: Compositions and Criticisms of Power,* edited by Charles W. Kneupper, 205-211. Arlington TX: Rhetoric Society of America, 1989.

Bryan, Ferald J. "Henry Grady, Southern Statesman," In *American Orators Before 1900: Critical Studies and Sources,* edited by Bernard K. Duffy and Halford R. Ryan, 197-204. Westport CT: Greenwood Press, 1987.

Campbell, J. Louis. "In Search of the New South." *Southern Speech Communication Journal* 47 (Summer 1982): 361-88.

Clark, E. Culpepper. "Henry Grady's New South: A Rebuttal from Charleston." *Southern Speech Communication Journal* 41 (Summer 1976): 346-58.

Erlich, Howard S. "Populist Rhetoric Reassessed: A Paradox." *Quarterly Journal of Speech* 63 (April 1977): 140-51.

Fulmer, Hal W. "Southern Clerics and the Passing of Lee: Mythic Rhetoric and the Construction of a Sacred Symbol." *Southern Communication Journal* 55 (Summer 1990): 355-71.

Gunderson, Robert G. "The Calamity Howlers." *Quarterly Journal of Speech* 26 (October 1940): 401-11.

Lindsay, Charles F. "Henry Woodfin Grady, Orator." *Quarterly Journal of Speech Education* 6 (April 1920): 27-42.

Metheny, David L. "The New South: Grady's Use of Hegelian Dialectic." *Southern Speech Communication Journal* 31 (Fall 1965): 34-41.

C. Newspapers

Atlanta Constitution. 13 February 1881.

Atlanta Constitution. 26 April 1886.

Atlanta Constitution. 17 August 1886.

Atlanta Constitution. 28 October 1888.

Atlanta Constitution. 26 June 1889.

Atlanta Constitution. 26 July 1889.

Boston Evening Transcript. 13 December 1889.

Dallas Morning News. 28 October 1888.

New York Tribune. 22 December 1886.

D. Manuscripts

Henry W. Grady Papers, Special Collections Department, Emory University, Atlanta.

Thomas E. Watson Papers, Southern Historical Collection, University of North Carolina, Chapel Hill.

E. Dissertations

Bauer, Marvin G. "Henry W. Grady: Spokesman of the New South." Ph.D. dissertation, University of Wisconsin, 1937.

Carageorge, Ted. "An Evaluation of Hoke Smith and Thomas E. Watson as Georgia Reformers." Ph.D. dissertation, University of Georgia, 1963.

Critical Perspective And Methodology

A. Books

Barrett, Harold, editor. *Rhetoric of the People*. Amsterdam: Rodopi, 1974.

Bergin, Thomas G. and Max H. Fisch. *The New Science of Giambattista Vico*. Ithaca: Cornell University Press, 1970.

Berlin, Isaiah. *Vico and Herder: Two Studies in the History of Ideas*. New York: Viking Press, 1976.

Black, Max. *Language and Philosophy*. Ithaca: Cornell University Press, 1949.

Black, Max. *Models and Metaphors*. Ithaca: Cornell University Press, 1962.

Edie, James E. *Speaking and Meaning: The Phenomenology of Language*. Bloomington: Indiana University Press, 1976.

Foss, Sonja K., Karen A. Foss, and Robert Trapp. *Contemporary Perspectives on Rhetoric*. Prospect Heights IL: Waveland Press, 1985.

Gusdorf, Georges. *La Parole*. Evanston: Northwestern University Press, 1965.

Hawkes, Terrence. *Metaphor*. London: Methuen, 1972.

Horner, Winifred B., editor. *The Present State of Scholarship in Historical and Contemporary Rhetoric*. Columbia: University of Missouri Press, 1983.

Johannesen, Richard L., Rennard Strickland, and Ralph T. Eubanks, editors. *Language is Sermonic: Richard M. Weaver on the Nature of Rhetoric*. Baton Rouge: Louisiana State University Press, 1970.

Kennedy, George A. *Classical Rhetoric and its Christian and Secular Tradition from Ancient to Modern Times*. Chapel Hill: University of North Carolina Press, 1980.

Lanham, Richard A. *A Handlist of Rhetorical Terms*. Berkeley: University of California Press, 1968.

Natanson, Maurice, and Henry W. Johnstone, editors. *Philosophy, Rhetoric and Argumentation*. University Park: Pennsylvania State University Press, 1965.

Ortony, Andrew, editor. *Metaphor and Thought*. Cambridge: Cambridge University Press, 1979.

Perelman, C. H., and L. Olsbrechts-Tyteca. *The New Rhetoric: A Treatise on Argumentation*, translated by Purcell Weaver and John Wilkinson. South Bend: University of Notre Dame Press, 1969.

Richards, I. A. *The Philosophy of Rhetoric*. London: Oxford University Press, 1936.

Richards, I. A. and C. K. Ogden. *The Meaning of Meaning*. New York: Harcourt Brace, 1930.

Roberts, Rhys. *The Rhetoric and Poetic of Aristotle*. New York: Modern Library, 1954.

Sacks, Sheldon, editor. *On Metaphor*. Chicago: University of Chicago Press, 1978.

Smith, Henry Nash. *Virgin Land: The American West as Symbol and Myth*. New York: Vintage Books, 1959.

Turbayne, Colin M. *The Myth of Metaphor*. New Haven: Yale University Press, 1962.

Weaver, Richard M. *The Ethics of Rhetoric*. South Bend IN: Gateway Editions, 1953.

White, Hayden. *Topics of Discourse: Essays in Cultural Criticism*. Baltimore: Johns Hopkins University Press, 1978.

B. Articles

Berthold, Carol. "Kenneth Burke's Cluster-Argon Method: Its Development and Its Application." *Central States Speech Journal* 24 (Winter 1976): 302-309.

Bormann, Ernest G. "Fantasy and Rhetorical Vision: The Rhetorical Criticism of Social Reality." *Quarterly Journal of Speech* 58 (December 1972): 396-407.

Brummett, Barry. "The Representative Anecdote as a Burkean Method, Applied to Evangelical Rhetoric." *Southern Speech Communication Journal* 50 (Fall 1984): 1-23.

Bryan, Ferald J. "Vico on Metaphor: Implications for Rhetorical Criticism." *Philosophy and Rhetoric* 19 (Winter 1986): 255-65.

Osborn, Michael. "Archetypal Metaphor in Rhetoric: The Light-Dark Family." *Quarterly Journal of Speech* 55 (April 1967): 115-26.

Osborn, Michael. "The Evolution of the Archetypal Sea in Rhetoric and Poetic." *Quarterly Journal of Speech* 63 (December 1977): 347-63.

Osborn, Michael, and Douglas Ehninger, "The Metaphor in Public Address." *Speech Monographs* 29 (August 1962): 223-34.

Stelzner, Herman G. "Ford's War on Inflation: A Metaphor that Did not Cross." *Communication Monographs* 44 (November 1977): 284-97.

Wrage, Ernest J. "Public Address: A Study in Social and Intellectual History." *Quarterly Journal of Speech* 33 (December 1947): 451-57.

Index

Abbot, Lyman 44
Absalom, Absalom! 17
Africa 141, 153
Agriculture: cotton prices 19, 53; cotton monopoly 51; crop diversity 51-52; crop-lien system 18-19, 53; foreign trade 84; Grady's views 52-57, 61-62, 108-124; "Virgin Land" 25; Watson's views 65-69, 71-72, 78-81, 84-86, 88, 151-153
Appomattox 23, 30, 101, 106, 120
Arnett, Alex Mathews 18
Arnold, Benedict 84
Aristotle 11, 75, 90
Athens, Georgia 32
Atlanta, Georgia 40-41, 59, 85, 113, 114
Atlanta constitution 2, 10, 40-43, 82, 99, 108
Atlanta Herald 40-41
Atlanta Sun 40-41
Augusta, Georgia 37, 64
Avery, Isaac W., 34
Baker, George F., 44
Babylon 120
Bannockburn, Battle of 139
Baptists 27, 36
"Black Friday" 133
Bauer, Marvin G. 6-7
Beauharnais, Josephine 64
Belisarius 120
Berlin, Isaiah 12
Bethany: A Story of the Old South: quoted 1; Watson's authorship 63
Bismarck, Otto 112
Bonaparte, Napoleon 64
Boston, Massachusetts 58, 59, 62, 114
Braden, Waldo 2
Brazil 85
Brewton, William 8
Brown, Joseph E. 113
Bullock, Rufus B. 39-40
Bunker Hill 104, 139
Burke, Edmund 126
Calhoun, John C. 22, 27-28, 30, 91, 113, 150
Calvin, John 126
Campbell, Louis 7
Canada 132
Carageorge, Ted 6
Cash, W. J. 10, 23, 30
Cavalier 45-47, 60-61, 90, 91, 100-101
Chicago, Illinois 116, 117, 129
Civil War 1, 84, 89, 90
Clark, E. Culpepper 7
Clay, Henry 113, 150
Cleveland, Grover 52, 59, 76-77, 95, 119
Cobb, Howell 113
Conkling, Roscoe 133
Connery, Thomas B. 41
Dallas, Texas 47-48, 85, 91
Darius 127
Davis, Harold E. 9
Davis, Jefferson 43
Dead Sea 133

Debating Societies 24, 32-34, 36-37

Declaration of Independence 79-80, 147

Democratic Party 17, 56, 76, 83, 84, 86, 88, 93

Dew, Thomas R. 21

Dickens, Charles 34, 128

Douglas, Ellen 134

Eaton, Clement 9

Edie, James 26

Ecroyd, Donald H. 4

Education: shortened school terms 20; "field schools" 20; Epideictic as education 75-76

Elberton, Georgia 55, 57, 92, 93, 108

Elections, Presidential: 1888 election 47, 76-77; 1892 election 68-69, 86; 1896 election 5, 6, 86; 1904 election 5; violence during 43-44

Elisha 124

Eloquence 36-37, 66; "Goddess of Eloquence" 66

Emmet, Robert 139

Emory College 28

England 117, 135, 148

English Common Law 143

Erlich, Howard S. 5

Fahvestock, H. C. 44

Faulkner, William 17

Finch, N. P. I. 42

Fort Sumter 32

France 132, 146, 148

French Revolution 78-79, 145-147

Furman, Richard 21

Gaines, Frances P. 39

Galileo 126, 142

Gaston, Paul 3, 8, 96-97

Georgia Courier 34, 39

Georgia State Fair 84-86

Goodwyn, Lawrence 97

Grady, Henry W.: "Against Centralization" (University of Virginia) speech 53-55, 93; as orator 1, 32-34; attacked by Watson 78, 81, 84-86, 88, 95; Bay State Club speech 59-60; Boston trip 58-60; Boston Merchants Association speech 58-59; comparison to Watson 72-73, 76, 78, 81, 88, 91, 92, 93-94, 96-98; early life 32-34; Dallas trip 47-52; debating societies 32-34; editor of Atlanta constitution 41-42; education at University of Georgia 32-33; education at University of Virginia 33-34; "Farmer and the Cities" (Elberton, GA) speech, analysis 55-57, 93, and text 108-124; journalism career 34, 39-44; "New South" speech, analysis 44-47, 92, 93, quoted 1, and text 99-107; metaphors summarized 60-62, 89-97; "Texas State Fair" (Dallas) speech, analysis 47-52, 91; radical views 48-52, 57-62, 93-94

Grattan, Henry 139

Gravlee, G. Jack 5-6, 95

Grant, Ulysses S. 23, 106, 120

Great Chain of Being 22, 29, 31, 49-50, 91

Greensboro, Georgia 70-72, 87

Gunderson, Robert 4
Gusdorf, Georges 89, 96
Haggard, Henry "Rider" 141,
	153; author of *She* 141
Hamilton, Alexander 79, 92
Hampden, John 138
Harper's Magazine 42, 53
Hart, Brett 34
Harris, Joel Chandler 10, 42
Harris, Nathaniel E. 63
Harrison, Benjamin 52
Hawkes, Terrence 11
Hayes, Rutherford B. 17
Hercules 125
Hill, Benjamin H. 43; quoted by
	Grady 1, 44-45, 99
Hicks, John D. 1
Hobson, Fred 31
Hood, John B. 82
Howell, Evan P. 41
Illinois 114
Inman, John H. 44
Iowa 114
Ireland 114-115, 127, 129
Italy 135
Kansas 114
Knox, John 126
Kossuth, Lajos 139
Ku Klux Klan 40
Jackson, Andrew 11, 92
Jackson, "Stonewall" 139
Jefferson, Thomas 11, 25, 79-80,
	92, 113, 147, 149
Jim Crow laws 43
Johnston, Joseph E. 104
Lamar, L. Q. C. 133
Lane, Mills 8
Lease, Mary Elizabeth 4
Lee, Robert E. 75-76, 87, 91,

	106, 108, 120, 139
*Life and Speeches of Thomas E.
	Watson, The* 125, 141
Lincoln, Abraham 45, 90, 104,
	113, 133
Lincolnton, Georgia 82-83
Lindsley, Charles F. 6
Lodge, Henry Cabot 58
London, England 111, 115
Louis XVI, King 121
Luther, Martin 126
McDuffie County, Georgia 34-35,
	64
McDuffie Journal 64
McLaws, W. R. 37
Macon, Georgia 84, 125
Massachusetts 103
Mason Dixon Line 103
Mecca 139
Mercer High School 67-68
Mercer University 35-37, 63, 87,
	95, 125
Metaphor, theory of: Aristotle's
	view 11; J. Edie's view 26,
	31; general use 10; I. A.
	Richards's view 12-14;
	Richard Weaver's view 24-
	25, 26; G. Vico's view 12
	Metaphorical criticism 14-15,
	24-26
Methodist Episcopal church 27
Michigan 110, 129
Milledgeville, Georgia 77, 95,
	141
Mirabeau, Honre Gabriel Victor
	126
Mississippi River 133
Missouri River 133
Mixon, Herald D. 7

Moore, Thomas V. 22
Morgan, J. Pierpoint 44
Moses 77
"Munchausen" 128
Myths 8, 96-97
Nashville Advocate 30
Necker, Jacques 121
New England 100, 105
New England Society of New
    York City 44, 99
New South Creed 7, 82-83, 96-97
New York City 44, 84, 99, 114,
    117
New York Herald 41
New York Tribune 43
Newton, Isaac 126, 142
Noah 100
Norman Conquest 143
O'Connell, Daniel 148
Ohio 110, 116
Ohio River 133
Osborne, Michael 15-16
Osterweis, Rollin 3
Oxford, Georgia 28
Palmer, Bruce 11
Pearce, R. H. 64
People's Party 5, 95
Penfield, Georgia 67, 87
Pennsylvania 103
Philip, King 127
Piedmont region 63
Pilgrims 44
Plymouth Rock 44
Poland 127
Pompey 127
Populism 4, 5, 8, 97
Puritans 45-47, 61, 90, 100-
    101, 135
Reconstruction Era 10, 17, 34,

39-40, 43, 51, 96
Religion: and slavery 28-29; and
    metaphor 27-29; "God's
    Chosen People" 23; Hugue-
    nots 135; post-Civil War 20-
    21; materialism as sin 22, 29;
    denominational splits 21, 27
Republican Party 40, 43, 50, 57,
    58, 61-62
Reynolds, W. C. 65
Rhetoric: 3; Epideictic (cere-
    monial) rhetoric 69-79;
    Eulogy 69-70; Forensic
    rhetoric 65
Richards, I. A. 12-14, 25
Richmond County, Georgia 64
Rome, Italy 135
Rome Commercial 40
Rome, Georgia 34
Rothschilds 133
Russia 116, 118
Samaria 124
Sea of Galilie 134
Sherman, William T. 18, 23, 44,
    82, 102-103, 104
Slavery 28, 105
Smith, Henry Nash 25
Smith, Hoke 6
Smith, John 100
Smith, Robert W. 4
"Southern Demagogues" 5, 95-96
Southern Farmer's Alliance 53,
    55, 58, 86
Southern oratory: surveyed 3; key
    to power 24
Spain 142
St. Clair-Abrams, Alexander 40
Stephens, Alexander H. 22, 35,
    69-70, 91, 113, 133

Stuart, Charles Edward 134
Sumner, Charles 133
Sydney, Sir Philip 134
Talmage, T. DeWitt 44, 101
Tammany Hall 99
Tariffs 72, 76, 86
Tate, Allen 89
Texas 110
Texas State Fair 47
Thermopylae, Battle of 127
Tindall, George 1
Thomson, Georgia 34, 37, 63, 64, 66
Tom Watson: Agrarian Rebel 8
Toombs, Robert 27-29, 30, 66, 91, 104, 111, 113, 133
"Uncle Remus" 109
Union Point, Georgia 65
University of Georgia 32-33
University of Virginia 33-34, 53-54
Vanderbilt, Cornelius 118
Vico, Giambattista 11-12
Virginia 100, 102
Vermont 103
Wallace, Sir William 127
Warrenton, Georgia 83-84
Watson, Ann 37
Watson, Thomas E.: as orator 1, 36-37; attacks on banking 68, 71-72; birthplace 34; *Bethany*, quoted 1; comparisons with Grady 72-73, 76, 78, 81, 82-86, 88, 91, 92, 93, 96-98; debating societies 36-37; early life 34-35; education at Mercer University 35-36; elections, presidential, 1888 election 76-77, 1896 election 5, and 1905 election 5; eulogy for Alexander Stephens 69-70; "Gallispaen Society" speech 66-67; Georgia State Fair Address (Macon, GA) 84-86; "Greensboro Georgia" speech 70-72; Grady's "New South" speech attacked 82-86, 88; legal practice 64-66; *Life and Speeches of Thomas E, Watson, The* 125; Lincolnton, Georgia speech 82-83; Mercer University (Macon, GA) Address, analysis 73-76, 87, 95, and text 125-140; Milledgeville Academy Address, analysis 77-82, 95, and text 141-153; People's Party 5, 95; Penfield, Georgia speech 67, 87; "Solid South" metaphor 82-83, 84-86, 88; Union Point, Georgia Address 65-66; Warrenton, Georgia speech 83-84
Weaver, Richard M. 24-25, 30-31, 89
Webster, Daniel 113, 150
Weld, Theodore Dwight 21
White, William A. 22
William and Mary College 21
Wilson, Charles Reagan 23
Wisconsin 129
Woodward, C. Vann: *Tom Watson:Agrarian Rebel* 8; views of Watson 2, 11, 95-96
Yazoo Land Fraud 132